D1707264

Easy Review™

for

Criminal Procedure

By

Randy J. Riley, *J.D.*
Seton Hall Law School

Contributing Editor

Brett E. Lewis, J.D.
Brooklyn Law School

Law Rules Publishing Corporation
Old Tappan, NJ 07675

(800)371-1271

Editorial Staff
Jared S. Kalina, *J.D.* Cardozo School of Law
Daniel P. Kinsella
Blair C. Pieri

Library of Congress

ISBN 1-887426-36-1

Note: This review publication is not meant to replace required texts as a substitute or otherwise. This publication should not be quoted from or cited to. It is meant only to be used as a reminder of some subject matter and is not a substitute for a comprehensive understanding of the actual materials which it references or outlines.

TABLE OF CONTENTS

I.   Incorporation

The Bill of Rights in our Constitution protects against violation of our rights by our federal government. The Supreme Court has one by one sought to enforce these rights against state governments. This process of making the rights protected by the Bill of Rights applicable to the states is known as incorporation. Not all of the Bill of Rights have been incorporated to the states. In this chapter, we review what rights have and have not been incorporated to the states through the Fourteenth Amendment.

A .   Approaches to Incorporation

1. Selective Incorporation
    a. This approach asserts that only those rights considered to be fundamental should be incorporated under the due process clause of the Fourteenth Amendment.

    b. It is only necessary to have fundamental fairness in a criminal trial.

    c. This approach is favored by the Supreme Court.

2. Total incorporation
    a. Believers in total incorporation argue that the Fourteenth Amendment incorporates all of the rights in the United States Constitution.

    b. This view has never been adopted by the Supreme Court

3. Total incorporation plus
    a. Believers in incorporation plus argue that rights other than the Bill of Rights should be incorporated to the States.

    b. For example, the right to a clean environment should be incorporated to the states.

    c. This view has never been adopted by the Supreme Court.

4. Case by case Incorporation
    a. Believers in the case by case approach analyze all of the facts in a particular case and then determine if there is a right involved.

    b. The problem with this approach is that the rights incorporated would be unpredictable and very subjective.

B. **Fundamental Rights**

1. Definition: The court has defined fundamental rights as those "of the very essence of the scheme of ordered liberty" and "principles of justice so rooted in the traditions in conscience for people as the ranking is fundamental." *Palko v. Connecticut*, 302 U.S. 319 (1937).

2. Rights held to be fundamental and incorporated:
    a. First amendment rights of freedom of religion, speech, assembly, invitation for redress of grievances.

    b. Forth Amendment rights relating to unreasonable arrest, search, and seizure.

    c. Fifth Amendment protections against self incrimination and double jeopardy.

    d. Sixth Amendment right to counsel, speedy trial, public trial, confronting a witness, and the right to produce witnesses.

    e. Eighth Amendment prohibition against cruel and unusual punishment.

3. Rights not incorporated
    a. Grand jury indictment.

    b. Prohibition against excessive bail and fines.

II.   Court Procedures

In this chapter we review the actual process of a criminal prosecution. We will start with pre-trial procedure, proceed to the trial and then post-trial procedures. We emphasize the framework and logistics of an actual prosecution.

A.   **Procedure before the trial.**

    1. Complaint is filed by victim or police.

    2. Arrest

    3. Booking

    4. Initial Appearance
        a. Review of arrest procedures.

        b. Re-informed of rights.

        c. Bail set or jail.

    (Grand Jury if state allows)

    5. Preliminary Hearing
        a. Determination of probable cause.

        b. Review evidence to "hold over for trial."

    (File the Grand Jury proceeding)

6. Arraignment
    a. Read charges in open court;

    b. Defendant gives plea:
        (i)   Guilty.
        (ii)   Not guilty.
        (iii) *Nolo Contendere* - "no contest." The defendant accepts the punishment without actually pleading guilty. Not every state allows this action. This is beneficial to a defendant because a plea of no contest prohibits its introduction as evidence in a related civil action.

    c. Plea bargain
        The defense or the prosecution may seek a plea bargain - that is where the defendant will plead guilty to a lesser crime in exchange for a lesser sentence.

B. **Trial Procedures**

1. *Voir Dire* - selection of jurors by questioning.

2. Challenges
    a. For Cause - e.g., during *Voir Dire* a question arises as to whether a particular juror could be fair and honest in judging the case (i.e., an African-American is on trial and the prospective juror says that she is prejudiced). A party may make an unlimited number of these challenges.

    b. Peremptory Challenge - each side gets so many juror dismissals without a reason. These are usually limited by law. These dismissals can not be used to cause under-representation of a particular minority class.

3. Opening Statements
    a. Prosecution

    b. Defense (can wait until they begin their rebuttal).

4. Prosecution Presents Evidence
    a. Direct examination of witnesses, if any, by prosecution.

    b. Cross-examination of witnesses, if any, by defense - testimony limited by what was said in the direct examination.

    c. Redirect of witnesses by prosecution - limited to testimony stated during cross-examination.

    d. Redirect of witnesses by defense - limited to testimony stated during redirect.

5. Prosecution closes.

6. Motions by the Defense.
    a. Motion for Acquittal - prosecution failed to establish elements of crime charged.

    b. Mistrial - may be made at any time. The evidence presented, witness testimony or prosecutorial action is so prejudicial that a fair trial would be impossible.

7. Defense Presents case.
    a. May make opening statement if none made at beginning of trial.

    b. Same procedure as in the Prosecution presentation, but roles are reversed.

8. Rebuttal evidence by the Prosecution.

9. Closing Arguments
   a. Prosecution

   b. Defense

10. Judge instructs jury.

11. Jury Deliberations

12. Verdict

C. **Post-Trial Procedures**

1. Motions to Overturn

2. Sentencing

3. Renewed Motions

4. Appeal

III. What is Search? What is Seizure?

The Fourth Amendment prohibits unreasonable searches and seizures. The Amendment was designed to protect persons and their things from arbitrary rule by the government. This chapter examines what is a search and what is a seizure, the remedies for an unlawful search or seizure, and the case law produced by the Supreme Court on this issue.

Fourth Amendment:
The right of the people to be secure in their persons, houses, papers and effects, against *unreasonable* searches and seizures shall not be violated, and no Warrants shall issue, but upon probable cause, supported by Oath or affirmation, and particularly describing the place to be searched, and the persons or things to be seized. (Emphasis added).

A. Definitions

1. **Search** - any type of governmental intrusion into an area in which a person has a "reasonable expectation of privacy." This not only includes homes, but any number of places where a person has a reasonable expectation of privacy. A person may have a reasonable expectation of privacy in a place for some purposes, but not for others. For example, while a person may reasonably expect that police are not electronically eavesdropping on a phone call that that person is having in a telephone booth, a person who lights up a big fat joint (marijuana cigarette) and smokes it in a glass booth has no reasonable expectation of privacy.

   Katz v. U.S., 389 U.S. 347 (1967)
   Facts: The FBI, without a warrant based on probable cause, attached an electronic listening device to a public telephone booth. Katz's conversation was taped. The taped conversation was used as evidence to secure a federal conviction for wagering.

Held: The placing of an electronic listening device on the outside of a telephone booth constitutes a *search* for the purposes of the Fourth Amendment. Katz had a reasonable expectation of privacy in the phone booth. Therefore, the wire tap was in violation of the Fourth Amendment right to be free from *unreasonable* searches and seizures. The intrusion need not be physical to be violative of privacy.

2. Seizure - any exercise of dominion or control by the government over a person or property.
   a. E.g., when the police arrest somebody, that is quintessentially a *seizure*.

3. Seizable Items
   a. Contraband;

   b. Evidence of crime (i.e., clothing, car, etc.);

   c. Fruits of the crime (i.e., money, stolen purse, etc.);

   d. Instruments of crime (i.e., weapons).

   e. Suspects.

B. **Search and Seizure (With a Warrant):**

Requirements of a Valid Warrant:
   1. Probable cause (no warrant shall be issued on less than probable cause);

   2. Officer's oath;

   3. Place to be searched and things to be seized stated with particularity; and

   4. Signed by a detached and neutral magistrate.

1. **Probable Cause**

   a. Defined - exists when "the facts and circumstances within the officers' knowledge and of which they had reasonably trustworthy information are sufficient in themselves to warrant a man of reasonable caution in the belief that an offense has been committed." *Brinegar v. U.S.*, 338 U.S. 160 (1949).

   b. Experience of the officer may be taken into account.

   c. Corroboration of Information

      Draper v. U.S., 358 U.S. 307 (1959)
      Facts: An informant who had proved to be reliable in the past gave police information about the defendant. The informant stated that the defendant would be traveling by train to another city on September 5th and returning on September 8th or 9th with 3 ounces of heroin. The informant gave a detailed physical description of the defendant and gave a description of the defendant's "habits." The police set up surveillance at the train station. On the 9th of September the police observed the defendant who matched the description given by the informant. The police arrested him and found 865 grams of heroin in his coat pocket. The defendant was arrested and found guilty.

      Held: Information received from an informant that is corroborated by police investigation can be sufficient to provide probable cause for an arrest. The Court noted that this type of hearsay is inadmissible in court but can be used to establish probable cause for an arrest or search.

d. Informants

Aguilar v. Texas, 378 U.S. 108 (1964), *overruled in part by Illinois v. Gates, infra* (for analysis *see* Modern Approach, *infra*).
Facts: Police officers approached a magistrate for a search warrant based solely upon an affidavit that recited the following: Affiants have received reliable information from a credible person and do believe that heroin, marijuana, barbiturates and other narcotics and narcotic paraphonelia are being kept at the above described premises for the purpose of sale and use contrary to the provisions of the law. The search warrant was issued.

Held: The search warrant should not have been issued because the affidavit did not provide a sufficient basis for a finding of probable cause. The Court articulated a two-prong test which remains important to probable cause determinations, though it is no longer the law. *See Gates, infra.*

The *Aguilar* two-prong test provided that the constitutional requirement of probable cause could be satisfied by hearsay information. The Court considered the following factors in making probable cause determinations based on hearsay information under *Aguilar*:
  (i) The reliability of the informant's information (or *basis of knowledge*).
  (ii) The credibility of the informant (or *veracity*).

Traditional Interpretation of Aguilar
Each prong was separate and independent. To establish probable cause police had to demonstrate that both factors were satisfied. (Reliable informant + reliable information). If one prong failed, there would be no probable cause.

Modern Interpretation of *Aguilar*

The Court in *Illinois v. Gates,* replaced the *Aguilar* "two-prong test with a "totality of the circumstances" test. Under the *Gates* totality standard, a deficiency in either prong of the *Aguilar* test can be overcome by a strong showing in satisfaction of the other prong.

Spinelli v. U.S., 393 U.S. 410 (1969)

Facts: Spinelli was convicted of conducting interstate gambling activities. The evidence presented by the government against Spinelli at trial consisted of items which were seized pursuant to a search warrant obtained by the FBI. The warrant was issued upon the sworn statement of an FBI agent. The agent stated that (1) defendant was seen crossing a bridge between Illinois and St. Louis, Missouri on 4 of 5 days; (2) defendant parked his car in a lot used by residents of a certain apartment building and was seen entering a particular apartment in the building that had two phones registered to a Grace P. Hagen; (3) Spinelli was a known bookie and gambler; and (4) the FBI had been informed by a "credible and reliable informant" that defendant was operating a gambling operation by means of the telephones in the apartment registered to Grace P. Hagen.

Held: The informant's tip and subsequent corroboration by FBI agents were not sufficient to provide a basis for a finding of probable cause. The Court noted that the first two allegations asserted in the warrant reflected only innocent-seeming activities. The third item was just a "bald and unilluminating assertion of suspicion" that is entitled to no weight in court. Lastly, when measured against the two-prong *Aguilar* test, the informant's information lacked indicia of reliability, and perhaps more importantly, the affidavit failed to set forth the basis for the informant's knowledge.

Illinois v. Gates, 462 U.S. 213 (1983)

Facts: The police received an anonymous tip in a handwritten letter that the defendants were selling drugs. The tip identified the defendants as Mr. and Mrs. Gates, told police where they lived, and described how the couple obtained the drugs that they sold. Mrs. Gates would drive the family car down to Miami and leave it for Mr. Gates to fill up with drugs and drive back to Illinois. Mrs. Gates would fly back home after she dropped the car off in Florida. The letter stated that Mrs. Gates would be driving down to Florida on May 3rd, and that Mr. Gates would be driving the car back North with $100,000 worth of drugs in it. The letter also stated that the Gates' currently had $100,000 worth of drugs secreted in their basement. The police learned that Mr. Gates had booked a flight to West Palm beach on May 5th. Agents surveiled Mr. Gates and observed him board the May 5th flight, check into a hotel room registered to Mrs. Gates, and then depart early the next morning in a Lincoln Mercury bearing the license plates of a station wagon registered to Mr. Gates. The driving between West Palm Beach and Bloomington, Illinois where the Gates' lived, was between 22 and 24 hours. The police officer in charge of the investigation signed an affidavit setting forth the foregoing facts and submitted it to a magistrate who determined that there was probable cause to issue a warrant. The Gates' car was searched, 350 pounds of marijuana was found in the trunk, and the Gates' were arrested. The Supreme Court of Illinois held that the evidence found pursuant to the search warrant had to be suppressed because the police lacked probable cause based on the anonymous letter and the corroborative evidence, to believe that a crime had been committed.

Held: The anonymous letter, together with police corroboration, set forth sufficient facts to establish probable cause. The Court abandoned a strict adherence to the two-prong *"Aguilar-Spinelli"* test in favor of a "totality of the circumstances" test. The "totality" test relies on the magistrate to make a "practical, common sense decision when given all the circumstances set forth in the affidavit before her, including the *veracity* and basis of knowledge of persons supplying hearsay information, that there is a *fair probability* contraband or evidence of a crime will be found in a particular place."

Net: (To wrap up the above cases). While *Aguilar - Spinelli* is no longer the law, the process employed by a magistrate under *Gates* is still largely the same as required by *Aguilar - Spinelli*. A magistrate, in making a probable cause determination, is still going to ask questions about the veracity and basis of knowledge of an informant. However, on review, the determination of a magistrate will receive greater deference.

e. Probable cause can never be established after the fact, but must exist before an officer executes a search or seizure. Any evidence seized in an after-the-fact situation would be inadmissible in court.

f. The following may contribute to a finding of probable cause:
   (i) Criminal record of suspect;
   (ii) High crime area;
   (iii) Admissions;
   (iv) Suspects flight from officers;
   (v) Suspicious conduct;
   (vi) Resemblance of suspect to the description of the perpetrator;
   (vii) Failure to answer officers questions.

g. Stale Information - if the police wait too long from the receipt of information to search a premises, the ensuing search and seizure will be illegal.

Sgro v. United States, 287 U.S. 206 (1932)
Held: The Supreme Court held that there was no probable
cause to search for illegal liquor in a hotel where an affidavit
alleged that the sale of beer took place three weeks earlier. The
information on which the warrant was obtained was stale.

2. Officer Oath

    a. Affidavit to a magistrate.

    b. Must contain more than conclusions.

    c. Independent information to allow the magistrate to judge on
       own whether probable cause exists.

3. The Particularity Requirement

    a. A warrant must with particularity describe the *place* to be
       searched and the *things* to be seized.
        1) Place to be searched:
           (i) Must describe the house, address, apartment
              number, etc., to be searched. Judged by the
              availability of information the officers had at the
              time they sought the warrant.

Maryland v. Garrison, 480 U.S. 79 (1987)
Facts: The police obtained a warrant on probable cause to
search McWebb's third floor apartment for drugs. When the
police sought and executed the warrant, they reasonably
believed there was only one apartment on the third floor.
Only later did the officers learn that they had really searched
two apartments. The police uncovered drugs in the second
apartment, and arrested McWebb's neighbor, Garrison, who
was convicted.

Held: A search warrant satisfies the particularity requirement when issued to police officers who, at the time the warrant was issued and executed, reasonably believed that one apartment occupied the entire floor of a building. Thus, the search was not in violation of Garrison's Fourth Amendment rights. The Court noted that the validity of the warrant must be judged in light of all the information that the police had at the time they sought the warrant.

Note: This case also can be viewed along with the good faith exception to the exclusionary rule cases. Here, the police made a good faith reasonable mistake in designating the second apartment as a place in which the police had probable cause to believe there were drugs. Nonetheless, because of the officers' good faith mistake, the court would not exclude the evidence.
　(ii)　May be necessary to label the room or area of place to be searched.

　b.　Things to be seized:
　　　(i)　Police cannot "go fishing" for evidence.
　　　(ii)　Need to describe items to be seized with particularity (i.e., Panasonic stereo, red 1997 Mustang convertible, photographs of nude Congress persons, cocaine).

　　Rationale:　This is to stop someone who obtains a warrant to seize an elephant in a barn from searching a desk in a house.

4.　Signed by a detached and neutral magistrate.

　a.　Can be someone other than a magistrate as long as that person is detached and neutral, AND is authorized to do so.
　　　(i)　Law Clerk
　　　(ii)　Court Administrator

    b. If not detached and neutral then the warrant is no good and any evidence seized would be inadmissible.

        (i) A Sheriff cannot be authorized to write warrants for searches and seizures because sheriffs are not neutral and detached.

        (ii) Prosecutors or investigators are not neutral and detached.

Lo-Ji Sales, Inc. v. New York, 442 U.S. 319 (1979)
Held: Magistrate can NEVER accompany police into the field on a determination of probable cause. Here, the magistrate, by accompanying the police, was no longer detached and neutral.

Coolidge v. New Hampshire, 403 U.S. 443 (1971)
Held: The attorney general of a state is not a detached and neutral magistrate. Therefore, the AG cannot issue warrants.

C. Other

1. Time Allowed for Search
    a. Not indefinite.

    b. Case-by-case analysis.

    c. As long as the situation warrants.

2. Anticipatory Search Warrant
    a. Definition: a warrant based on probable cause that items to be searched or seized will be at a certain place at a certain time.

    b. FBI Law Enforcement Bulletin:
Where officers have probable cause to believe that evidence or contraband will arrive at a certain location within a period of time, they need not wait until delivery before requesting a

warrant. Instead, the officers may present an application for probable cause to a magistrate before the arrival of the evidence, and the magistrate can issue an anticipatory search warrant based on probable cause that the evidence will be found at the location to be searched at the time the warrant is executed.

   c. If the contingency upon which probable cause was granted does not occur then the warrant is void.

3. Standing to Challenge

   a. Only a person whose Fourteenth Amendment rights have been violated has *standing* to challenge a search. A person has standing to assert a Fourth Amendment violation only if she has a reasonable expectation of privacy in the things to be searched.

   b. A person does not have a reasonable expectation of privacy in:
   (i) A friend's car (*see Rakas v. Illinois*, 439 U.S. 128 (1978)), or
   (ii) A girlfriend's purse (*Rawlings v. Kentucky*, 448 U.S. 98 (1980).

Note: The touchstone is the *reasonableness* of the expectation of privacy. These cases all turn on their facts. For example, it might be reasonable for an overnight guest to harbor an expectation of privacy, but more so for a weekly visitor. If the guest sleeps on a couch in a heavily trafficked part of the home, his expectation of privacy might be less than if he had his own room.

The Court made clear in *Rawlings*, however, that a *possessory* interest in an item, alone, is not sufficient to give rise to a reasonable expectation of privacy.

Minnesota v. Carter, No. 97-1147 (1998)
Facts: A police officer suspected the defendant of being a local drug dealer. The officer looked into the defendant's apartment through a window. The window blinds were closed except for a small gap, which the officer peered through. The officer saw the defendant, Carter and Johns bagging cocaine. The officer arrested the defendant and the friends. At trial, Carter and Johns moved to suppress the evidence as an illegal search and seizure. The trial court held they were not overnight social guest and therefore did not have standing to object to the illegal search. The State Supreme Court reversed and held that Carter and Johns did have standing because they had a legitimate expectation of privacy in that situation.

Held: The Supreme Court reversed. The Court held that the search did not violate the Fourth Amendment. The Court noted that the State Supreme Court ruling was expressly rejected in *Rakas v. Illinois, supra.* The Court indicated that overnight guests do have a right of privacy but every guest. A person merely present in a house even with consent does not automatically enjoy that expectation. The Court also noted that the situation was commercial in nature: a drug transaction. The Court opined that the only reason Carter and Johns were there was to complete a business transaction. The Court noted that since the visit was business oriented that in itself leads to a lower expectation of privacy.

City of West Covina v. Perkins, No. 97-1230 (1998)
Facts: Police obtained a search warrant of the defendant's premises. The police executed the warrant when the defendant was not a home. The police seized property as a result of the search. The police left a notice form specifying the facts of the search, its date, the searching agency, the warrant's date, the issuing judge and his court, the person to contact on the seized items, and an itemized list of property seized. The police failed to leave the warrant number. The defendant sought the return of

the seized items and failed. The federal district court granted summary judgment for the city. The Ninth Circuit reversed holding that the Due Process Clause required that the respondents be provided a detailed explanation and procedures of how to recover the seized property, including the warrant number and the method for obtaining a copy of the warrant.

Held: The Supreme Court reversed the Ninth Circuit decision. The Court articulated that the Due Process Clause does not require the State provide a detailed explanation and procedures for the property's return. The Court criticized the Ninth Circuit's expansive view of the Due Process Clause.

IV. Stop and Frisk

If police officers could not stop and question a suspect on less than probable cause, the effectiveness of the police would be curtailed. Yet, allowing police officers to stop and question suspects on nothing more than a hunch would interfere with the Fourth Amendment right to be free from *unreasonable* searches and seizures. In many situations, the police lack probable cause to act, yet are able to articulate a reasonable suspicion, something more than an "inchoate hunch," that a suspect has committed or is about to commit a crime. In *Terry v. Ohio*, the Supreme Court held that a stop on less than probable cause could be Constitutionally *reasonable*.

A. Reasonable Suspicion

Terry v. Ohio, 392 U.S. 1 (1968)
Facts: Officer McFadden, a 39 year veteran of the Cleveland Police Department, noticed Terry and another man acting in a suspicious manner. Terry and his companion were taking turns walking past a storefront window and peering in. From his experience as a police detective, Officer McFadden gathered that Terry and his companion were "casing" the store. Officer McFadden approached the suspects and asked for their names. When one of them mumbled something, Officer McFadden grabbed Terry and spun him around, and then proceeded to pat down the outside of Terry's clothing. Officer McFadden felt a pistol, and Terry was arrested for possession of a concealed weapon.

Held: The Police may stop a suspect on less than probable cause upon a reasonable suspicion that the suspect has committed or is about to commit a crime. An officer may then frisk a suspect if the officer reasonably suspects that the suspect is carrying a concealed weapon. These types of stops and searches on less than probable cause are commonly known as "Terry Stops."

United States v. Cortez, 449 U.S. 411 (1981)
Held: Police must have "a particularized and objective basis" for suspecting that the person stopped has engaged in criminal activity.

20

1. What is a Stop?

> *United States v. Mendenhall*, 446 U.S. 544 (1980)
> **Facts:** DEA Agents, relying on a drug courier profile, approached Mendenhall in an airport and asked to see her identification and airline ticket. The name on Mendenhall's ticket did not match the name on her identification. When the agents questioned Mendenhall on her travel plans, she became "extremely nervous." Mendenhall agreed to accompany the agents to a nearby office where she consented to a search of her person. The agents found drugs during a strip search, and Mendenhall was arrested.
>
> **Held:** The Court held that Mendenhall was not "seized." The agents did not use force or brandish any weapons, most of the questioning took place in a public place, and the defendant consented to the agent's requests. Mendenhall was "free to leave" at any time.
>
> **Rule:** *A person is seized when, in light of the circumstances, a reasonable person would have believed that she was no longer free to leave.*

a. Drug Courier Profiles

1) An officer's observations may properly be supplemented by *drug courier profiles* detailing modes or patterns of operation.

2) Drug courier profiles may provide the police with sufficient information to make a *stop*, but not an *arrest*.

> *United States v. Sokolow*, 490 U.S. 1 (1989)
> **Facts:** The defendant fit the DEA drug courier profile: he paid for tickets with $20 bills; he traveled under a false name; his destination was Miami, an illicit source for drugs; he checked none of his luggage; he stayed in Miami for only 48 hours; and

he appeared nervous during his trip. DEA agents, relying on the drug courier profile, stopped the defendant and detained him just long enough to allow a drug sniffing dog to sniff the defendant's luggage. The dog made a positive "hit" for cocaine, and defendant was arrested.

Held: The drug courier profile, in this case, provided the DEA agents with reasonable suspicion upon which to base an investigative stop.

b.   Anonymous tips, when corroborated, may give police reasonable suspicion that a crime has been or is about to be committed.

Alabama v. White, 496 U.S. 325 (1990)
Facts: The police received an anonymous tip that a woman would be leaving a certain room in an apartment complex, getting into a brown car with a broken taillight and driving toward Dobey's Hotel with an ounce of cocaine inside a brown briefcase. The police set up surveillance and observed the defendant leave the room in the apartment complex and get into a car matching the given description. They pulled her car over just before she reached Dobey's Hotel. Defendant consented to a search of her car, inside which the police found a briefcase containing marijuana and cocaine. Defendant was arrested and convicted. She appealed on the grounds that the police did not have reasonable suspicion to stop her car.

Held: While the tip, alone, was not sufficient to create reasonable suspicion, the tip was corroborated by the fact that the things alluded to in the tip largely occurred. The cumulative happening of events from the tip was substantial enough to create reasonable suspicion.

c. When Does a Stop on Less Than Probable Cause Become an
    Unconstitutional Arrest?

   1. Duration
      (i)   A stop may only last as long as is necessary under
             the circumstances.

             United States v. Place, 462 U.S. 696 (1983)
             Facts: Place and his luggage were detained at an
             airport by police upon suspicion that he was
             transporting drugs. Place was held for 90 minutes
             while the police waited for a trained drug sniffing dog
             to arrive. The dog, upon being exposed to the
             luggage, made a positive identification for cocaine.
             Place was arrested and convicted.

             Held: Officers may temporarily detain a suspect and
             his luggage for exposure to a dog trained in detecting
             narcotics on the basis of a reasonable suspicion that
             the luggage contains narcotics. Also, exposing
             luggage to a dog trained in narcotics detection is not a
             "search." The Court found, however, that 90 minutes
             was too long a period of time for such a detention on
             less than probable cause. Thus, it was
             constitutionally *unreasonable* to hold Place for 90
             minutes on reasonable suspicion alone.

             Note: In assessing whether a detention is too long,
             it is appropriate to examine:
             (1) Whether police pursued a means of investigation
             likely to confirm their suspicions quickly; and
             (2) It must be *necessary* to detain the defendant.

(ii) The reasonableness of a stop is judged on a case-by-case basis.

Florida v. Royer, 460 U.S. 491 (1983)

Facts: Royer matched a drug courier profile. After purchasing a one way ticket and checking in his luggage, Royer was approached by two police detectives. The detectives asked to see Royer's driver's license and airline ticket, which Royer produced. The names on the ticket and the identification did not match. During the ensuing conversation, Royer became noticeably more nervous. The officers did not return Royer's identification or his ticket, but requested that he accompany them to a detention room located about forty feet away. One of the detectives, without his permission, took Royer's baggage check stubs and retrieved his luggage. Royer was then asked if he would consent to a search of his suitcases. Royer produced a key to one of the suitcases which contained drugs. Royer was arrested and convicted.

Held: By the time that Royer produced the key to his suitcase, the detention to which he had been subjected was a more serious intrusion on personal liberty than is permissible on mere *suspicion* of criminal activity. What had begun as a consensual inquiry in a *public* place had turned into an investigatory procedure in a police interrogation room. The detectives had Royer's ticket, they had his identification, and they had his luggage. At no time was he informed that he was free leave. The Court also found that there was no reason that trained dogs could not have been used to search Royer's luggage while in the public concourse. Thus, Royer had been unreasonably and impermissibly seized on less than probable cause.

Note: There is no hard and fast rule with regards to how long a stop can last or when a permissible stop on reasonable suspicion turns into an impermissible seizure on less than probable cause. These cases are fact-specific.

Florida v. Bostick, 501 U.S. 429 (1991)
Facts: Police officers brandishing guns entered a bus. On less than reasonable suspicion, the officers asked defendant if he would consent to a search of his luggage. The defendant consented and the police found drugs.

Held: Defendant was free to leave the bus at any time, but chose to remain of his own desire to travel. A person is not seized simply beacuse a police officer approaches him and asks a few questions. So long as a reasonable person would feel free to disregard the police and go about his business, the encounter is consensual and no reasonable suspicion is required. Here, defendant was not "seized" by the police.

United States v. Sharpe, 470 U.S. 675 (1985)
Facts: A DEA agent on patrol noticed a pickup truck with an attached camper traveling in tandem with a car. The truck was riding low and a quilted material covered the windows of the camper. The agent called for backup and a local police trooper responded to the call. When the trooper signaled to the car to pull over, the pickup truck cut between it and the trooper's car, nearly striking the latter. The trooper pursued the truck while the agent approached the Pontiac, which had pulled over, and requested identification. The trooper stopped the pickup truck, and waited 15 minutes for the agent to arrive. After securing the situation at the car, the agent arrived at the site of the pickup truck. He soon after smelled an odor of marijuana and searched the back of the truck. The occupants of the car were arrested 30-40 minutes after they had been detained.

Held: There is no absolute hard and fast time limit for *Terry* stops. As long as the police pursue a means of investigation that is likely to confirm or dispel their suspicions quickly, a detention of a suspect is appropriate. In this case, the suspects contributed to the delay by their actions.

(iii) *Pursuit* is not a seizure.

California v. Hodari D, 499 U.S. 621 (1991)
Facts: When approached by police and asked for identification, defendant ran and threw away a crack vial. The police recovered the vial of crack cocaine and arrested the defendant.

Held: Anything dropped or thrown away by a suspect prior to their seizure by police is considered to have been abandoned, and is not subject to protection under the Fourth Amendment. *There is no seizure until the suspect is under physical control.* Thus, a person, to be seized, must either be *apprehended* or *submit to authority*.

Note: Long detention of a suspect is allowed if there is a reasonable suspicion that the suspect is smuggling drugs internally.

B. Frisk

1. An officer may *frisk* a suspect on less than probable cause only if the officer reasonably suspects that the suspect is carrying a concealed weapon.

2. May only "pat down" the outer clothing of the suspect.
    a. If an object feels like a weapon it may be seized, even if it later turns out not to be a weapon.
    b. If the item does not feel like a weapon, it cannot be seized.

3. If probable cause is established during a Terry stop then the stop may become a valid arrest.
    a. Police may then search:
        (i) The person of the arrestee, and
        (ii) The area within the immediate control of the arrestee ("The grabable area.")

C. Stop and Frisk in the Immigration and Border Seizure Context

1. Police may stop a car on reasonable suspicion that it is carrying illegal aliens.

2. Suspicionless border checkpoints are proper.

    United States v. Martinez-Fuerte, 428 U.S. 543 (1976)
    Held: A fixed check-point border search without reasonable suspicion is proper in light of the states' interest in regulating the influx of illegal aliens into their jurisdictions.

3. Border/Customs agents at airports do not need to have reasonable suspicion to search belongings.

4. It is constitutionally impermissible randomly to stop Latinos in a roving border patrol search, (*see Almeida-Sanchez*, 413 U.S. 266 (1973)) or to stop a car full of Mexicans 25 miles from the border on the basis of race alone. (*See United States v. Broznoni-Ponce*, 422 U.S. 873 (1975)).

    • More on border highway regulation.

5. When police stop a car on *reasonable suspicion*, they can subsequently search the inside of the car if they have a reasonable fear that the person or persons inside the car may be armed. The search of the passenger compartment of an automobile, limited to those areas in which a weapon

may be placed or hidden, is permissible if the police officer possesses a reasonable belief based on specific and articulable facts which, taken together with the rational inferences from these facts, warrants the officer in believing that the suspect may gain immediate control of weapons. (*See Michigan v. Long* 463 U.S. 1032 (1983)).

6. It is no further intrusion on privacy rights to ask the driver of a car pulled over for a traffic infraction to get out of the car than to remain. *Pennsylvania v. Mimms*, 434 U.S. 106 (1977).

Deleware v. Prouse, 440 U.S. 648 (1979)
Held: In the absence of reasonable suspicion that either a vehicle or its occupant is subject to seizure for violation of the law, stopping a driver to check her license and registration is unreasonable under the Fourth Amendment.

Michigan Dept. of State Police v. Sitz, 496 U.S. 444 (1990)
Held: Sobriety checkpoints that stop every car, or every third car, etc., pursuant to fixed police guidelines are *per se* reasonable under the Fourth Amendment. The Court found that states have a compelling interest in preventing drunk driving, while the intrusion on privacy visited upon motorists by fixed check-point stops is slight.

Note: *Sitz* allows police to stop cars with *no* suspicion whatsoever as long as the method chosen by the police follows guidelines that minimize police discretion, and the stops are not random.

V. Exclusionary Rule

Central to constitutional criminal procedure is the Exclusionary Rule. The Rule requires suppression of illegally obtained evidence. This Rule has been applied to violations of the Fourth, Fifth, Sixth and Fourteenth Amendments. This Rule is unique to American Jurisprudence. In this section, we will explore the rationale, definition, operation of and cases involving the Exclusionary Rule.

A. Generally

1. Evidence obtained by the government in violation of a Constitutional right is not admissible in a court of law to prove guilt.

2. Purpose
   a. Maintain judicial integrity.

   b. Deter bad conduct on the part of law enforcement officers.

   c. Protection of person's constitutional right to privacy.

3. Source of Exclusionary Rule
   a. Judge Made - not from Congress or the Constitution.

   b. Used only in criminal proceedings.

4. Applies to state as well as federal courts.

   Mapp v. Ohio, 367 U.S. 643 (1961)
   Held: The Exclusionary Rule not only applies to the federal courts but also to the state courts. Thus, any evidence obtained in violation of a person's Fourth and Fourteenth Amendment rights must be excluded.

5. Procedure for Invocation
    a. Pre-trial motion

    b. Burden on prosecution

B. What is not Admissible?

1. Illegally seized evidence

2. "Fruits of the Poisonous Tree"
    a. Definition - any evidence that is the direct or indirect
        result of the initial illegal search or seizure. (e.g., a
        confession may be the fruit of an unlawful arrest).

    b. All evidence from the resulting illegal act is inadmissible in
        court, unless it has been obtained by means sufficiently
        distinguishable to be purged of the primary taint.

    c. For example, officers unlawfully arrest Mary Juana and
        unlawfully search Mary Juana's home without a warrant.
        Surprisingly, they find drugs. The drugs would be
        inadmissible in court because the warrantless search of Mary
        Juana's home, absent exigent circumstances, violates her
        Fourth Amendment right to be free from unreasonable
        searches and seizures. The officers also find a day planner
        which says "pick up 1000 kilos of cocaine at 101 High
        Street." The police go to 101 High Street and seize 1000
        kilos of cocaine. That cocaine would be excluded as fruit of a
        poisonous tree, unless the prosecution could successfully
        argue that there would have been:
        (i)   *Inevitable discovery* of the evidence;
        (ii) There was an *independent source* for the
              information; or
        (iii) There was sufficient *attenuation.*

C. **Exceptions to the Exclusionary Rule**
(Burden of proof on Prosecution.)

1. Inevitable Discovery

   a. Fruit of a poisonous tree is admissible if the court finds that the evidence would have been discovered anyway by lawful means.

   b. Usually limited to physical evidence or weapons.

      Nix v. Williams, 467 U.S. 431 (1984)
      Facts: The police obtained statements from the defendant in violation of his right to counsel. Those statements lead the police to the body of a 14 year old girl. The defendant was convicted of murdering the girl, but the Supreme Court overturned the conviction. During a second trial, the prosecution sought to use evidence of the body, location, and other crime scene evidence to show defendant's guilt. The defendant contended that such physical evidence should be excluded as a fruit of the illegally obtained statement.

      Held: The body and evidence were admissible under the doctrine of inevitable discovery since they would eventually have been found even absent the illegal statements. The Court noted that the reason for the exclusionary rule is that the government should receive no advantage from illegal police actions. Here, however, police would have found the evidence anyway so there is no real benefit that would come from excluding the evidence.

      The Burden of Proof: The prosecution must prove by a preponderance of the evidence that the evidence would have been discovered by other means.

2. To determine whether there is sufficient *attenuation* to cleanse an illegal arrest of its taint, look at:
   a. The *flagrancy* of the illegal conduct;

   b. The *temporal proximity* between the arrest and confession; and

   c. The presence of *intervening circumstances.*

3. Purged Taint
   a. Intervening actions, including defendant's own acts, remove the taint of an illegal act.

   b. Defendant's act must be:
      (i) Voluntary;
      (ii) Made after the stress of the original taint has dissipated.

   Wong Sun v. United States, 371 U.S. 471 (1963)
   Facts: The police illegally searched Toy's apartment. As a result of the search Toy made an incriminating statement against Yee. The police obtained heroin from Yee, who said that it came from Toy and Wong Sun. Wong Sun was charged and taken into custody, and released. Seven days later Wong Sun confessed. The question presented to the Court was "whether granting the establishment of the primary illegality, the evidence to which instant objection is made has been come at by exploitation of that illegality, or instead by means sufficiently distinguishable to be purged of the primary taint."

   Held: The Court held that Wong Sun's confession days after the illegal search of Toy's apartment was so attenuated as to dissipate the taint.

Brown v. Illinois, 433 U.S. 590 (1975)
Held: Statements made inside two hours after illegal arrest were inadmissible fruits of a poisonous tree, despite the intervention of *Miranda* warnings.

4. Relationship between confession and illegal entry into a home.

   Rule: Once a defendant leaves the threshold of the home, any confession he makes is *unrelated* to the illegal entry.

5. There is a legal distinction between *physical evidence* and a *live witness*.

   United States v. Ceccolini, 425 U.S. 268 (1978)
   Facts: An officer stopped to talk to a friend who was an employee at a local flower shop. While there the officer unlawfully opened an envelope containing money and gambling slips. The officer's friend told him that it belonged to the defendant. The officer relayed the information to the FBI. Months later, the FBI questioned the friend who was willing to testify against the defendant.

   Holding: For attenuation purposes, there is a distinction between *physical evidence* and *live witnesses*.

   Note: The Court's treatment of live witnesses can be explained by its theory that live witnesses, unlike physical evidence, possess free will. Even in the absence of the illegal search, it is possible that a live witness *could* come forward and testify, whereas physical evidence never volunteers to be found.

6. Independent Source

> Evidence is admissible if the prosecution can prove that it could have been obtained by an independent and lawful source, wholly unconnected to the illegal search and seizure.
>
> *U.S. v. Crews*, 445 U.S. 463 (1980)
> **Facts:** Defendant was identified as a possible suspect in a pair of bathroom robberies at the Washington Monument. Unable to photograph the defendant at the scene, police took him into custody, questioned him, and took his photograph. A victim later identified the defendant from the illegally obtained photograph.
>
> **Held:** A defendant is not, himself, a suppressible "fruit" and the illegality of his detention does not deprive the government of the opportunity to prove his guilt through the use of untainted evidence. In this case, the police had an independent basis to suspect defendant's involvement in the crimes with which he was charged - eyewitness identifications.

7. The *independent source* rule also applies where police have probable cause to search a premises, but no warrant.

> *Murray v. United States*, 487 U.S. 573 (1988)
> **Facts:** Police entered premises unlawfully, with no warrant but upon probable cause, found drugs, and then left. The police then applied for a warrant to search the premises, but did not mention that they had previously searched them. The police went back and seized the drugs.
>
> **Held:** Police had an *independent source* upon which to get a warrant, so the evidence came in.

8. Good Faith exception to the Exclusionary Rule
   a. Requirements
      - (i)   Police *reasonably* rely on warrant issued by detached and neutral magistrate;
      - (ii) That is later found to be defective.

   b. Consequence - Physical evidence that meets the requirements of the exception is admissible in the prosecutor's case-in-chief.

   > ***United States v. Leon***, 468 U.S. 897 (1984)
   > **Facts:** The police obtained a search warrant based upon an informant's tip and police investigation. The police executed the warrant finding drugs and other evidence used to convict the defendant. Later, the search warrant was found to be deficient of probable cause. As a result, the defendant argued that the evidence obtained using the defective warrant should have been excluded. The government argued that because the officers acted in good faith, there should be an exception to the Exclusionary Rule.
   >
   > **Held:** *Evidence obtained in reasonable reliance on a subsequently invalidated search warrant is admissible.* The Court noted that one reason for the Exclusionary Rule is to curb violative police conduct. When officers act in good faith there is no danger of illegal police conduct. Most importantly, the Court found that the exclusion of evidence in this situation would have no significant deterrent effect on the issuing magistrate. Remember that if an affidavit was falsely used to gain a warrant then the Good Faith Exception is not available.

   c. Applies to:
      - (i)   Overturned cases;
      - (ii) Overturned rulings;
      - (iii) Subsequent changes in the law;
      - (iv) Finding of new Constitutional rights.

D. **Exclusionary Rule Inapplicable in Following Proceedings**

1. Private searches where the evidence is turned over to the government by a non-government searcher;

2. Civil Proceedings;

3. Post-conviction sentencing;

4. Grand Jury investigations;

5. Impeachment proceedings.

6. Parole Revocation Hearings

Pennsylvania Board Of Probation and Parole v. Scott, No. 97-581 (1998)
Facts: A condition of the defendant's parole was that he was to refrain from owning or possessing weapons. Parole officers believed he was violating this rule. The officers searched his home without a warrant and found firearms and bows and arrows. The State sought to revoke the defendant's parole. The defendant sought to suppress the evidence. The Hearing Examiner denied the motion. The Commonwealth Court reversed, which was affirmed by the State Supreme Court. The court held that, although normally the Fourth Amendment does not play a role in parole revocation hearings, it does in the instant case because the officers in control of the search was aware of the defendant's status as a parolee. The court reasoned that to hold otherwise would not deter officers from randomly searching paroled criminals at will.
Held: The Court concluded that the Exclusionary Rule does not bar the introduction of evidence seized in opposite of the Fourth Amendment at a parole revocation hearing. The Court noted that the Rule is judicial created and not applicable in every situation.

The Court opined the social aspects of allowing a parolee out of jail and under restrictions outweighs any alternative. The Court also noted that there is a high percentage of repeat offenders among parolees. An officer in this situation need not be deterred.

E.   Rationales for the Exclusionary Rule

1.   Prevents violators of constitutional rights from "profiting" from their misconduct.

2.   Deters misconduct by government personnel.

3.   Preserves the integrity of the judicial system.

4.   Protects right to privacy.

5.   Leads to greater training and professionalism in law enforcement.

6.   Necessary if Fourth Amendment Right to be free from unreasonable searches and seizures is to have any meaning.

F.   Reasons Militating for the Elimination of the Rule

1.   Guilty persons may be set free because of over-zealous law enforcement.

2.   Encourages police to commit perjury.

3.   Diminishes overall respect for the justice system.

4.   Does not punish the violator of the constitutional right - it punishes society by freeing guilty parties.

5. United States is the only country which has this type of rule ("Fruits of the Poisonous Tree").

7. The Exclusionary Rule is not explicitly required by the Constitution.

G. **Alternatives**

1. Allow evidence to come in but allow person to sue government in tort for violations.

2. Hold the individual officer who violates Constitutional rights accountable in tort or provide for disciplinary action.

3. Expand the Good Faith Doctrine, *see supra.*

H. **History Lesson**

Alternatives to the exclusionary rule, such as those listed above, *have failed* in the past to provide adequate safeguards for Fourth Amendment rights.

VI. Arrest

The Fourth Amendment protects individuals from unlawful searches and seizures. An arrest is the quintessential "seizure" within the meaning of the Fourth Amendment. Thus, the Fourth Amendment protections extend to arrests. This chapter will examine the nature, scope, and limitations of what an arrest is, including the amount of force that can be used and the constitutional ramifications of arrest.

A. **Definition**
An arrest is the taking of a person in custody against their will for the purpose of criminal prosecution.

B. **With a Warrant**

1. Issued by a detached and neutral magistrate, upon probable cause, describing with particularity the person to be seized (*see* "warrants" under search and seizure below).

2. Description of person is sufficient as long as that description reasonably identifies the accused at the time of the arrest.

3. A warrant may be served only within the state or jurisdiction of its issuance.

4. Time served
   a. Felonies - anytime.

   b. Misdemeanors - daylight hours usually.

5. Announcement Requirement
   a. Most state statutes require that an officer *announce* her purpose and authority before entering a home without permission.

   b. Exceptions:
      (i)   Danger to police;
      (ii) Third persons are in danger;
      (iii) Crime in progress;
      (iv) Strong possibility that evidence is being destroyed.

U.S. v. Ramirez, No. 96-1469 (1998)
Facts: A reliable informant told an officer that he saw a dangerous escaped prisoner at the respondent's home. The officer then observed a man walking into the home resembling the escaped fugitive. The officer obtained a "no-78 knock" warrant to enter and search the respondent's home. The officers rushed the home breaking windows and doors. The respondent believing he was being burglarized pulled a gun and shot it in the air to scare the would be burglar. The police then announced their agency and he immediately lowered the gun. After admitting he owned and fired the gun and that he was a convicted felon (not the escaped prisoner) he was arrested. He was arrested for felon in possession of a firearm. The district court granted a motion to suppress the evidence because there was no exigent circumstances to justify the no-knock and the breaking of personal property. The Ninth Circuit Court of Appeal affirmed.
Holding: The Supreme Court reversed. The Court noted that the Fourth Amendment does not hold officers to a higher standard actions when the warrant is a "no-knock" warrant. The Court articulated that the standard is whether the police have a reasonable suspicion that an announcement would be dangerous or futile. Reasonable suspicion does not depend on whether property must be damage. The Court realized that property damage must be reasonable to search. The Court opined that unreasonable property damage may violate the Fourth Amendment. However, the Court pointed out that windows

and doors were damaged. In this type of situation, the door was for entry of the officer and the windows allowed outside officers to "cover" the entering officers and prevent any person from getting and using a weapon. This was reasonable.

6. Other Ways to Arrest
   a. Citation

   b. Summons

C. Warrantless Arrest

1. Most arrests are made without a warrant.

2. Arrest for Felonies:
   a. On probable cause to believe that a suspect has committed or is about to commit a felony.

   b. May arrest suspect in a public place.

   c. Can not enter a private home without an arrest warrant, absent exigent circumstances:
      (i)   Hot pursuit.
      (ii)   Risk of danger to the police or others.
      (iii) The need to prevent a felon's escape.

Payton v. New York, 445 U.S. 573 (1980)
Facts: The police had probable cause to believe that the defendant had committed a murder. Without a warrant the police went to Payton's apartment. They knocked on the door but there was no answer. They opened the door with a crowbar and entered the home. There was no one home. In plain view, however, there was a gun shell casing matching

the type of weapon used in the murder. The evidence was admitted at trial and the defendant was convicted.

Held: Justice Stevens emphasized that the house is an especially private place deserving of special protection. In the absence of exigent circumstances the police may not enter a home without a warrant. Therefore, the shell casing should not have been admitted into evidence.

3. Arrest for Misdemeanors
   a. In the officers presence.

   b. No entry into the home.

D . Post-Arrest

1. Full body search of the accused.

2. "Wingspan" or "grabable area" search (*see* search and seizure, *infra*).

3. Inventory search (*see infra*).

E . Force in Arrest

1. The reasonableness of a particular *seizure* depends not only on when it was made, but on *how* it was carried out.

2. Deadly Force - level of force that a reasonable police officer would conclude carries a high risk of death or serious bodily injury, regardless of whether actual death occurs.

   a. ONLY allowed in Felonies, NEVER misdemeanors.

Tennessee v. Garner, 471 U.S. 1 (1985)

Facts: Police were dispatched on a "prowler" call. When the police officer arrived on the scene he saw the complainant gesturing to the back yard. The officer went to the back in time to see a person running toward a fence. The officer stated that he was reasonably sure that the suspect was unarmed. He identified himself as an officer and told the suspect to stop. The suspect began to climb the fence. Believing that the suspect would escape, the officer shot him. The suspect, an unarmed 14 year old boy, later died of the gunshot wound inflicted by the police officer.

Held: The use of *deadly force* can be an *unreasonable seizure* unless a police officer has probable cause to believe that:
- (i) A suspect poses a risk of *serious injury or death* to the officer or others; or
- (ii) The suspect is armed.

  b. Basic Guidelines
- (i) Suspect committed a violent crime; or
- (ii) Is armed with a deadly weapon.

Note: If possible, the officer should give warning that deadly force will be used.

3. The police may use non-deadly force in arresting a suspect, but only to the extent that use of force would be reasonable under a totality of the circumstances.
   a. Police may use force:
   - (i) On suspects resisting arrest;
   - (ii) For the protection of officers or third parties;
   - (iii To prevent escape or to recapture a fleeing suspect.

4. Civil Liability of Officers

   Graham v. Connor, 490 U.S. 386(1989)
   Held: The Supreme Court ruled that any claim of excessive force (deadly or not) is to be governed by the reasonableness standard of the Fourth Amendment. The Court noted that the following factors should be considered in a determination of whether excessive force was used:
       (i) The severity of the crime;
       (ii) The nature of the offense; and
       (iii) The extent of the resistance.

VII. Search and Seizure (Without a Warrant)

A. **Exceptions to the Warrant Rule**

1. Stop and frisk (discussed *supra*);

2. Search incident to arrest;

3. Consent;

4. Exigent circumstances;

5. Automobile exception;

6. Plain view/open fields doctrines;

7. Administrative search;

8. Inventory search.

1. Stop and frisk - discussed *supra*.

2. Search incident to arrest

    a. Three issues arise under the search incident to arrest doctrine:
        (i) What types of arrests justify a search incident?
        (ii) When may such a search be undertaken?
        (iii) What is the *reasonable* and permissible scope of these searches.

b.   Police may search area within immediate control of suspect.

Chimel v. California, 395 U.S. 752 (1969)
Facts: The police obtained a warrant for the arrest of the defendant on charges of burglarizing a coin shop. The police traveled to the defendant's house and waited inside with the defendant's wife for the defendant to return. When he entered the home he was shown the arrest warrant and was asked if the police could look around. The defendant objected, but the police stated that based upon the arrest warrant, they could conduct a search of his home. No search warrant had been issued. The entire house was searched from top to bottom including drawers and such. The entire search lasted approximately an hour.   The police found evidence which they used to convict defendant.

Held: The search was unlawful. Upon a valid arrest, only the person arrested and the "area into which an arrestee might reach in order to grab a weapon or evidentiary item, or grabable area," may be searched without a warrant. The "grabable area" would include any area "within an arestee's immediate control."

c.   Arrest in an automobile
1)   May search the entire interior of the car including glove compartment.

2)   Cannot search the trunk.

3)   Can search trunk if car is hatchback type of vehicle.

4)   Can open closed containers in car (i.e., briefcase or brown paper bag in the backseat).

United States v. 222, 414 U.S. 218 (1973)

Facts: An officer who had investigated the defendant four days earlier had reason to believe, based upon that investigation, that defendant was operating a vehicle without a driver's license. The officer signaled defendant to stop his car. All of the occupants of the car ran except for the defendant-driver. The officer arrested defendant for the offense of driving without a license. The officer then performed a search incident to arrest, patting down the defendant's outer clothing. During this pat down, the officer felt "something" in the defendant's coat pocket. The officer could not tell what it was, so he reached into the pocket and pulled out a crumpled cigarette pack. The officer did not know what was in the pack, but he knew that it was not cigarettes. The officer then searched the pack and found heroin in capsule form. The defendant was convicted for possession and concealment of heroin. The appeals court overturned the conviction on the grounds of illegal search and seizure.

Held: *A person arrested incident to a lawful custodial arrest can be searched by police without regard to the substantive crime forming the basis of the arrest.* The Court confirmed that a search incident to a lawful arrest is a traditional exception to the warrant requirement of the Fourth Amendment.

d. The fact that the substantive legal basis for an arrest is a *pretext* does not matter.
   (1) Subjective intent, alone, does not make otherwise lawful police conduct illegal or unconstitutional.

Whren v. United States, 517 U.S. 806 (1966)

Facts: The police suspected Whren of committing a drug offense and used the traffic laws as a *pretext* to stop and search him for drugs.

Unanimously held: Once police arrest a suspect upon probable cause for violation of a substantive (traffic) offense, no matter how minor, they have a right to search the driver and the *passengers* incident to the arrest.

New York v. Belton, 435 U.S. 454 (1981)
Facts: An officer pulled over a car containing four persons for speeding. The officer asked to see the driver's license and registration. None of the persons in the car owned the vehicle or were related to the registered owner. Meanwhile, the officer had smelled marijuana and had seen in plain sight on the floor of the car an envelope saying "Supergold." He directed all of the occupants out of the car and arrested them for unlawful possession of marijuana. The officer then picked up the envelope and discovered marijuana. He then searched the passenger compartment of the car. On the back seat he found a leather jacket belonging to defendant. In a pocket the officer discovered cocaine. Defendant was arrested for possession of cocaine.

Held: *Any time an officer "has made a lawful custodial arrest of the occupant of an automobile, he may, as a contemporaneous incident to that arrest, search the passenger compartment of that automobile." The officer may also search any containers, opened or closed, within the area searched.*

Implication: The inside of a car is just one giant "grabable area."

Knowles v. Iowa, No. 97-7597 (1998)
Facts: Case involving search after a citation. The defendant was speeding. The police stopped him and wrote a citation for a motor vehicle infraction rather than arresting him. The police officer conducted a full search of the car without consent or probable cause. The officer found marijuana and a marijuana

48

pipe. The defendant moved to suppress the evidence as an illegal search and seizure. The State argued that this was a search incident to arrest. The defendant claimed that no arrest occurred and that a citation does not rise to the level of an arrest. The trial court denied the motion. The State Supreme Court affirmed the decision enunciating a bright line "search incident to citation" rule.

Holding: The Supreme Court stated that although State law authorized such a search it was in violation of the Fourth Amendment. The Court indicated that a citation situation does not rise to the level of an arrest. Therefore, the reasoning behind the search incident to arrest is inapplicable to a search incident to citation. The Court noted that the safety issue in a citation is a great deal less that it is with an arrest. The Court propounded that although a traffic stop may allow the officer to pull persons from a car, it does not allow for the greater and more intrusive search. The Court noted that it is possible that during an arrest, probable cause could enter and allow a full blown search. However, the Court held that did not occur in this case.

e. Contemporaneous with search

1) Very close in time to the arrest.

2) Even if suspect is under complete control of officer, police may still search.

3) If too much time has passed, then the fruits of the search are excluded.

4) A person arrested incident to a lawful custodial arrest can be searched by police without regard to the substantive crime forming the basis for the arrest.

United States v. Edwards, 415 U.S. 800 (1974)
Facts: Edwards was arrested for trying to break into a post office. He was booked and placed in jail close to midnight. The next morning the police seized his clothes and subjected them to a paint analysis after discovering that the person who had attempted to break into the post office had scraped paint chips off of a post office window. The results showed that paint on defendant's clothes matched the paint from the post office window. The defense contended that the search was too remote from the time of arrest to be a search incident to arrest, and therefore was unlawful.

Held: The search of an arrestee may take place at the time of the arrest or later at the place of detention. In this case, the Court found that the search was valid because "the normal process incident to arrest and custody had not yet been completed" with Edwards placed in his cell.

f. Expanding the search incident doctrine:

Maryland v. Buie, 494 U.S. 325 (1990)
Held: Police can make a protective sweep of a dwelling during the course of an arrest if the police have a *reasonable suspicion* that there is some danger. As an incident to arrest, the officers could, as a precautionary measure, and without probable cause or even reasonable suspicion, look in closets and other spaces immediately adjoining the place of arrest from which an attack could be launched. Beyond that, there must be *articulable facts* which, if taken together with *rational inferences* would warrant a reasonably prudent officer in believing that the area to be swept harbored individuals posing a danger to those on the arrest scene. The Court noted that the intrusion on privacy is slight when weighed against the safety of the officers.

Note: Police may not, as part of a protective sweep, search dresser drawers, file cabinets or other items not capable of hiding a would-be assailant.

g. Justifications
    1) Prevents escape;

    2) Officer safety;

    3) Stops destruction of potential evidence;

    4) Prevents concealment of weapons or evidence.

3.   Consent

a. Requirements:
    1) Voluntary; and

    2) Intelligent.

b. Voluntary
    1) Not the result of police force or threat.

    2) Question of fact to be determined from all circumstances.

    3) Silence is not consent.
    4) Scope of consent:
        (i) A person consents to only what they can be reasonably understood to have consented to.
        E.g., Consent to enter premises is not consent to search, and consent to search a locked car does not give police consent to break open a locked briefcase in the trunk of the car.

      (ii) The prosecution has the burden of proving that consent was freely given in each instance.

c. Intelligent
    1) Know that police are asking; not an undercover cop.

    2) Mental stability.

d. Warnings need not be given.
    1) You can have voluntariness even if people do not know that they have the right not to consent to a search.

e. Who may consent?
    1) Owner in possession - yes.

    2) Lessee - yes.

    3) Family Members - yes.

    4) Roommate - yes, but only as to those areas that the roommate and the suspect share (i.e., the common areas). The roommate cannot give permission to search any room (i.e., suspect's bedroom) in which the roommate does not have unfettered access.

    5) Any person who it is reasonable for the police to believe has a right to consent - yes. *(See Rodriguez, infra)*.

    6) Landlord - no.

    7) Hotel clerk - no.

    8) College/university administrators - no.

    9) Business employer/employee - no

    10) High school administrators - *see* special circumstances, *infra*.

Schneckloth v. Bustamonte, 412 U.S. 218 (1973)

Facts: A police officer pulled over a vehicle with a burned out headlight and license plate light. The driver had no license and only one of the six people in the car produced a driver's license. That man claimed to be the brother of the owner of the car. After the arrival of backup, the officer asked the person with the driver's license if he could search the car. The man said "sure, go ahead," and opened the trunk for the officer. The officer found three stolen checks. The defendant was arrested and convicted of possessing the stolen checks. The case came to the Supreme Court on review of a habeas decision reversing the affirmance of the defendant's conviction by the California State Supreme Court.

Held: Consent was freely given. A court's determination of whether consent was freely given or was the result of duress or coercion should be based upon a totality of the circumstances. A suspect's knowledge that she has the right to decline to consent to a search is but one factor in the determination of voluntariness. Thus, under the Court's formulation, a search may be "voluntary" even if a suspect is not given any warning that he or she has a right to refuse to consent to the search.

Illinois v. Rodriguez, 497 U.S. 177 (1990)

Held: If a 3rd party has *apparent authority* over a premises on which the police *reasonably rely,* and the 3rd party consents to a search, the search is reasonable.

E.g., a 3rd party represents to the police that she shares an apartment with the defendant. She produces a key and lets the Police into the apartment. In fact, she has not lived there in a month. The 3rd party appears to have *common authority* over the apartment, but in fact she has none. It is the *appearance* of authority that gives Police acting on the reasonable belief that the 3rd party, in fact, has common authority, the right to search the apartment without offending the Fourth Amendment.

4.   **Exigent   Circumstances**

    a. Need an emergency that would make getting a warrant impractical, dangerous, useless, or unnecessary.

    b. For example:
       1) Hot pursuit.

       2) Immediate danger to third party.

5.   **Automobile Searches on Probable Cause**

    a. **Rule** - The warrantless search of an automobile stopped by police officers who have probable cause to believe the vehicle contains contraband is not *unreasonable* within the meaning of the Fourth Amendment.

    b. Justifications:
       1) Mobility of cars;
       2) Diminished expectation of privacy in a vehicle;
       3) In plain view;
       4) Cars are highly regulated by the government;
       5) Constitutional difference between houses and cars.

Carroll v. U.S., 267 U.S. 132 (1925)
Held: *Cars may be searched upon probable cause without a warrant.* The Court noted that cars are mobile, and it would not be practicable for police to secure a warrant to search mobile vehicles because "the vehicle can be quickly moved out of the locality or jurisdiction in which the warrant must be sought."

c. Based on probable cause that seizable items are contained within a vehicle.
    1) May search interior of car.
    2) May search trunk and all containers inside of car. (*See Acevedo, infra*).

United States v. Ross, 456 U.S. 798 (1982)
Facts: The police received a tip from a reliable informant that the defendant was selling drugs out of the trunk of his car at 439 Ridge Street. The informant gave the police detailed descriptions of both the defendant and his car. The police found the defendant and the car where the informant said they would be. The defendant was arrested after one of the officers noticed a bullet in plain view and found a pistol in the car's glove compartment. Upon searching the trunk, the police opened a brown paper bag and found heroin. At the station the police made another warrantless search of the car and uncovered a leather pouch containing large amounts of cash. The government used this evidence to convict defendant of possession of heroin with intent to distribute.

Held: When the police have probable cause to search a car for contraband, they may search the entire car and any containers found within that car that could contain evidence of crime.

d. Auto exception applies to all motor vehicles such as motor homes, boats, trucks, cars, motorcycles, etc.

e. Abandoned cars - *can be searched for the limited purpose of determining ownership.* If an officer found drugs in the glove compartment of such a car while looking for the car's registration, then the drugs would be admissible against the owner of the car in a prosecution for possession of drugs. If, however, the officer found the drugs in a hidden compartment in the trunk, then the evidence would be excluded as the result of a constitutionally unreasonable search.

United States v. Chadwick, 433 U.S. 1 (1977)
Held: A locked footlocker seized in public may not be searched without a warrant.

Note: To the extent that *Chadwick* held that locked trunks in automobiles could not be seized without a warrant, that case has been *overruled* by *California v. Acevedo*. In *Acevedo*, the Court held that police may perform a warrantless search of luggage or locked containers found inside a car upon probable cause to search either the entire car or the locked container. *See California v. Acevedo*, 500 U.S. 565 (1991).

Implication: People now have a greater protection in the luggage and containers that they carry on the street than those which they place in a locked car.

6. **Plain View Doctrine**

   a. **Rule:** An officer must:
     1) Be lawfully where she is;
     2) The seizable nature of the items in question must be *immediately apparent*; and
     3) The officer may not do anything that qualifies as a search (i.e., moving and touching things).

   b. Within the sight of the officer
     Items must be visible without touching or moving them.

c.   In the place lawfully
Any place where police have a legal right to be. For example, police who chase a suspect into an apartment in "hot pursuit" may properly seize contraband in the apartment that is in "plain view."

d.   Immediately apparent that item is contraband.
1)   No further investigation or examination is necessary.

2)   Can "call in" serial numbers from items that the officer believes are stolen but may not pick up item to *search* for serial numbers that are not visible. (*See Arizona v. Hicks, infra*).

3)   Based on reasonable police experience.

Arizona v. Hicks, 480 U.S. 321 (1987)
Facts: The defendant discharged a weapon in his apartment. The police were summoned. When they entered the apartment they noticed a stack of expensive stereo equipment. Suspecting that the equipment was stolen, an officer picked up a stereo receiver and wrote down the serial numbers. When he called in the numbers he learned that the stereo had been stolen in an armed robbery. The defendant was arrested and convicted of armed robbery.

Held: The police officer engaged in an *unreasonable* search of the stereo equipment in violation of the defendant's Fourth Amendment rights. The police officer lacked probable cause to believe that the stereo had been stolen, and the serial number on the stereo equipment was not visible in plain view. The officer had to pick up the equipment and physically manipulate it until the serial number came into view. This he could not do.

Texas v. Brown, 460 U.S. 730 (1983)
Facts: A police officer stopped defendant's car during a routine driver's license checkpoint stop. The officer asked to see defendant's license, and at the same time shined a flash light into the car and saw the defendant drop what appeared to be a drug-filled balloon onto the floor of the car. When the defendant opened his glove compartment to look for his license, the officer, with the aid of the flash light, noticed several plastic vials and quantities of white powder.

Held: The use of a flashlight does not negate a plain view seizure. The Court stated that "the use of artificial means to illuminate a darkened area simply does not constitute a search, and thus triggers no Fourth Amendment protection."

Horton v. California, 496 U.S. 128 (1990)
Facts: An officer filed a warrant application that referred to the proceeds of a robbery and the weapons used. However, the warrant that was actually issued left out the weapons used in the robbery and only listed the three rings that were taken. Upon executing the search warrant, the officer did not find any of the rings, but did find the weapons in plain view. At trial the officer testified that he was searching for the rings, but that he was also interested in finding the weapons used in the robbery. The defendant was convicted and he appealed on the ground that the weapons should have been suppressed because their discovery was not *inadvertent*.

Held: The Constitution does not mandate the suppression of evidence found in plain view when that evidence's discovery was not inadvertent, i.e., when the police were looking for specific evidence not listed on a search warrant. The Court noted the characteristic of inadvertency is consistent with the discovery of evidence in plain view, but it is not a requirement of a plain view discovery.

e. Open Fields Doctrine
  1) Explanation: any item found in an open field is subject to seizure without probable cause or a warrant and is not protected by the Fourth Amendment. A person has no reasonable expectation of privacy in an open field. (*See Oliver v. United States, infra*).

  2) Very broad interpretation today.

Oliver v. U.S., 466 U.S. 170 (1984)
Facts: The police received a tip that the defendant was growing marijuana. They drove by his house and saw a locked gate with a No Trespassing sign. A path lead around the gate. The police followed the path several hundred yards to where they discovered an open field of marijuana.

Held: The protection of the Fourth Amendment extends only to the home and it's curtilage. The Court noted that there is a difference between a police entrance into a home and an entrance into a "open field." Displaying an obvious lack of style, the Court held that a person does not have a reasonable expectation of privacy in an open field. Fences and signs do not prevent people from seeing into an open field or the activities that take place in such a field.

  3) Not Open Fields:
     (i) House;
     (ii) Curtilage;
          Area immediately surrounding a dwelling or area associated with the dwelling which is protected by the Fourth Amendment.

     Examples: Garages connected to houses; area immediately surrounding house. A person has no reasonable expectation of privacy beyond the curtilage of the home. *See United States v. Dunn*, 480 U.S. 294 (1978).

4) Test for curtilage:
   - (i)   Proximity to the house;
   - (ii) Whether the area is in an enclosure with the house;
   - (iii) Nature and use of area;
   - (iv) Steps to conceal from public view. *See U.S. v. Dunn*, 480 U.S. 294 (1987).

5) Normal aerial surveillance of curtilage permitted.

California v. Ciraolo, 476 U.S. 207 (1986)
Facts: The police, suspecting drug activity, flew a plane at approximately 1,000 feet above the defendant's home and viewed the curtilage of the home. The curtilage was enclosed by a 6 foot outer and 10 foot inner fence so that the public could not see into the defendant's yard.
32
Held: There was no "search" within the meaning of the Fourth Amendment. The Court noted that even though the defendant went to great lengths to hide his property from the public's view, the defendant's expectation that people would not view his curtilage from the sky was *unreasonable.* The police and any other citizens had a right to be in that airspace. Thus, there was no Fourth Amendment violation.

Florida v. Riley, 483 U.S. 445 (1989)
Facts: The police hovered at approximately 400 feet above defendant's property in a helicopter while they observed his yard and curtilage. While hovering above defendant's greenhouse, the police spotted marijuana plants growing through a hole in the greenhouse roof.

Held: A plurality of the Court held that a person lacks a reasonable expectation of privacy in a residential backyard from the vantage point of a helicopter located 400 feet above. The Court noted that police may see what may be seen from where they have a right to be, helicopters and planes make routine use of the public airways, and the contents of defendant's greenhouse were visible from the air.

Note: Justice O'Connor, in her concurrence, stated that if a defendant can prove that the airways above his house are not "routinely traveled" by airplanes and helicopters, then he does have a reasonable expectation of privacy which has been violated by the police.

Dow Chemical Co. v. U.S., 476 U.S. 227 (1986) **Facts:** Facts are same essentially as in *Riley* except environmental violations were viewed from airplane. This time photographs were taken.

Held: No violation. The police had right, just as public did, to be in airspace.

7. **Administrative/Special Needs Searches**

a. These cases all involve searches other than for evidence of crime where the state has *special needs*.

b. In *Bell v Wolfsih*, 439 U.S. 816 (1979), the Court held that pretrial detainees retain some privacy rights, but that strip searches and body cavity searches were *reasonable*.

c. A convicted inmate has no legitimate expectation of privacy in a jail cell.

d. The warrantless search of the *home* of a probationer on reasonable suspicion is *reasonable* within the meaning of the Fourth Amendment.

Camara v. Municipal Court, 387 U.S. 523 (1967)
Facts: A statute allowed the warrantless search/inspection of houses for violations of the fire code. The defendant refused to allow such an inspection of his home.

Held: The Court, overruling *Frank v. Maryland*, 359 U.S. 360 (1959), held that while the Fourth Amendment protects against administrative searches, the need for the inspection must be weighed in terms of the reasonable goals of code enforcement. Probable cause to obtain inspection warrants exists where the proposed inspection is a *reasonable* intrusion on privacy.

New Jersey v. TLO, 469 U.S. 325 (1985)
Facts: A teacher walked into a bathroom and smelled cigarette smoke. The teacher suspected TLO, a student, of smoking. TLO denied that she was smoking. The school's Vice Principal searched TLO's purse for cigarettes but instead found rolling paper and marijuana which were used against TLO in a juvenile proceeding.

Held: A school is justified in performing a search of a student when there are "reasonable grounds" for suspecting that the student has violated or is violating the rules of the school.

Note: *Reasonable grounds* are something more than a hunch, yet something less than reasonable suspicion, and note that a student can be searched for a violation of a school's rules. Thus, without having violated a single law, a student can "reasonably" be searched under the Court's decision in *TLO*, and evidence obtained during such a search can be used against the student in a criminal or juvenile prosecution.

O'Connor v. Ortega, 480 U.S. 709 (1987)
Held: The Court unanimously rejected the contention that government employees can never have a reasonable expectation of privacy in the workplace. Yet, non-investigatory, work-related

intrusions are not Fourth Amendment violations, nor are *investigatory searches* for evidence of work related employee misfeasance.

New York v. Burger, 482 U.S. 691 (1987)
Facts: Pursuant to a state regulation, police officers conducted a warrantless inspection of defendant's junkyard. Defendant could not produce the required business license and "police book" of automobiles that were junked. The police then performed a search of the yard and copied several VIN numbers from junked cars. The police inspection revealed that several of the cars and parts from the yard had been stolen. The defendant was arrested and convicted of possession of stolen property.

Held: The Court upheld the statute and the conviction. The Court held that while the Fourth Amendment governs searches of commercial businesses, *the privacy interest in a "closely regulated" commercial business is less than the privacy interest a person has in a home.* A person who engages in this type of business must apply for a government license, follow stringent government regulations, adhere to proper bookkeeping methods, and know that the government makes routine inspections.

Rule: Warrantless inspections of commercial businesses must meet these criteria:
(i) *There must be a substantial government interest* that informs the regulatory scheme pursuant to which the inspection is made;
(ii) The warrantless inspections must be *"necessary to further [the] regulatory scheme"*; and
(iii) *The regulatory statute must perform the basic functions of a warrant:*
 (a) It must advise the owner that the search is being made pursuant to the law and has a properly defined scope, *and*

      (b) It must limit the discretion of the inspecting
officers.

Skinner v. Railway Labor Executives' Assoc., 489
U.S. 602 (1989)
Facts: The government passed legislation that in all train
accidents the conductor be tested for drugs. Following such an
accident, a conductor was tested for drug use. The test
revealed that the conductor had drugs in his system at the
time of the accident. That information lead to his
termination and to his criminal prosecution.

Held: The Court upheld the testing. Stating that the
government has a compelling special needs interest in train
safety which allows the warrant requirement to be bypassed in
the case of train conductor drug testing. In such a case, the
drug test and its procedures are reasonable within the meaning
of the Fourth Amendment. Without immediate action,
evidence could be lost through normal bodily functions - this
makes getting a warrant impracticable.
e. In *special needs* cases, the Court tells us that you do not need
   a warrant or probable cause so long as the request to search is
   reasonable at the outset, and the search is performed in a
   reasonable manner.
     • Court does not even require reasonable suspicion.

f. Taking urine for testing is a search

National Treasury Employees Union v. Von Raab,
489 U.S. 656 (1989)
Facts: Decided the same day as *Skinner*. Customs agents,
persons who carried firearms, and employees that handled
classified documents were all subjected to mandatory drug
testing under federal law. A person of the same sex monitored
production of urine samples. Anyone who tested positive had
to give a satisfactory explanation or be dismissed. The test

results could be used in a criminal prosecution of a customs employee.

Held: The Court upheld the suspicionless mandatory drug testing of drug agents and those who carry firearms. Here, it is the employee who voluntarily seeks a position which they know requires mandatory drug testing. The government has a special and compelling need to ensure that persons occupying these positions are not under the influence of drugs.

Vernonia School District v. Acton, 515 U.S. 646 (1995)
Verona School district implemented a policy of randomly testing the urine of its student athletes for drugs. A same sex monitor supervised the production of the samples at a distance of 12 to 15 feet while the students urinated in bathroom stalls.

Held: The Court held that it is *reasonable* for a school to perform random drug testing on its student athletes without a warrant, without probable cause, and without even reasonable suspicion. While the Court emphasized the importance of the school's interest in deterring drug use by its students, it noted that student athletes have a lesser expectation of privacy than the general student population:
   (i)   They suit up and shower in public locker rooms;
   (ii)   They sign waivers; and
   (iii) They undergo additional examinations.
Finally, the Court found that the privacy interests that were implicated were negligible because the urine samples were produced in the privacy of a bathroom stall.

8.   **Inventory Search**

   a. Inventory searches are a well defined exception to the warrant requirement.

   b. An inventory search satisfies the Fourth Amendment's reasonableness requirement as long as:
      1) Search is made pursuant to reasonable police regulations, and
      2) Administered in *good faith.*

   c. *Rationale*: This is supposedly done to protect owner's property and protect police from false claims.

   d. Anything maybe inventoried: cars, planes, bags, briefcases, wallets, purses, etc.

South Dakota v. Opperman, 428 U.S. 364 (1976)
Facts: Opperman's car was impounded by the police on a parking violation, and the police conducted a warrantless inventory search of the contents of the car. The police found marijuana in the glove compartment of Opperman's car. The search was conducted pursuant to standard police procedure and was found not to be arbitrary.

Held: The search was reasonable under the Fourth Amendment:
   (1) To protect valuables left in plain view on the dashboard of the car;
   (2) To protect the police against lost property claims; and
   (3) To protect the police and the public from dangerous items concealed in cars.

Note: The fact that the car had to be forcibly unlocked did not make the search unreasonable.

Illinois v. Lafayette, 462 U.S. 640 (1983)
Facts: The police conducted an inventory search at the police station of a shoulder bag belonging to a man arrested for disturbing the peace. The search uncovered drugs.

Held: The Court upheld the search. "It is not unreasonable for the police, as part of the routine procedure incident to incarcerating an arrested person, to search any container or article in his possession, in accordance with well-established inventory procedures."

Note: Justice Burger who wrote for the majority suggested that the government's interest in conducting an inventory search at the police station "may in some circumstances be even greater than those supporting a search incident to arrest." The inventory search conducted at a station house also provide a greater measure of privacy to the person being searched than does the on-the-street search incident to arrest.

Colorado v. Bertine, 479 U.S. 367 (1987)
Facts: The defendant was arrested for driving while intoxicated and his van was impounded. Well established police guidelines gave the police the discretion to lock defendant's van in a parking lot or drive it down to the police station and inventory its contents. The defendant's van was inventoried and evidence of crime was found in a closed backpack and nylon bag in the van. The evidence was used at trial to convict defendant.

Held: Police inventory regulations administered in good faith are constitutional. The Court noted that there must be written guidelines for an inventory search (the police cannot perform inventory searches on a case-by-case basis absent reasonable police regulations). This curtails the discretion of the officers to search at their leisure. Officers have a right to inventory items so that they are not subject to liability claims for missing items.

Note: Even though police regulations limit discretion, *Bertine* also tells us that it is Constitutionally reasonable for such a regulation to leave police officers with the discretion to decide when to conduct and when not to conduct an inventory search pursuant to that regulation.

VIII.   Privilege Against Self Incrimination

The Fifth Amendment guarantees that "no person shall be compelled in any criminal case to be a witness against himself. This language has not been interpreted literally. The Court has sought to balance personal privacy rights against abuse by police and government officials and the need for evidence in criminal trials. Witnesses forced to testify against their will may face "the cruel trilemma" of self incrimination, perjury, or contempt. Coerced or forced confessions and testimony are of dubious reliability, and even innocent witnesses may look guilty when subjected to a hostile cross examination. It is with these considerations in mind that this chapter explores what has come to be known as the "right against self incrimination."

A.   Privilege Against Self-Incrimination

1. "No person shall be compelled in any criminal case to be a witness against himself." - Trial of Aaron Burr.

2. The privilege kicks in when:
   a. A witness refuses to answer a question on the grounds that her answer might incriminate herself;

   b. A direct answer *may* actually incriminate the witness;

   c. A statement would provide *links* or *leads* to a future criminal prosecution.

3. Assertion of the privilege against self incrimination is an issue for the judge to decide.

4. The privilege also applies to grand jury proceedings.

5. Does a witness have a privilege in the face of a statute granting a witness *immunity* from prosecution? It depends on what the statute means by "immunity."

    a. Congress got into the act of passing immunity statutes that immunize witnesses from prosecution in exchange for their testimony.

    b. *Use immunity* assures only that testimony, itself, will not be used against a witness in a future criminal prosecution, or to obtain other evidence against the witness.

        Conselman v. Hitchcock, 142 U.S. 547 (1892)
        Held: An immunity statute, to be valid, must protect a witness against the *use* of his testimony against him to secure derivative evidence to be used against him at a criminal trial.

        Note: This type of testimonial immunity is known as "use" immunity. The witness' testimony cannot be *used* against him, but the witness may still be prosecuted on the basis of independent evidence.

    c. *Transactional immunity* affords a witness absolute immunity against future prosecution for the offense to which the questioning relates. E.g., in New York, if you testify before a grand jury, you are immunized as to the transaction or *offense* underlying the testimony.

        Note: The Supreme Court, in *Kastigar v. United States*, 406 U.S. 441 (1972), held that transactional immunity, while satisfying the Fifth Amendment right against self incrimination, is not constitutionally required. Use immunity is "coextensive" with the scope of the privilege against self incrimination, and therefore, is sufficient to compel testimony over a claim of privilege.
        Note: The Fifth Amendment permits, *but does not require*, transactional immunity.

6. You cannot ever compel a *defendant* to testify, nor even mention the fact that the *defendant* is not testifying.

7. Immunity
   a. Once immunity is granted the state cannot use testimony or any of its "fruits" to prosecute a witness. *Murphy v. Waterfront Commission*, 378 U.S. 52 (1964).

   b. The immunized witness may be forced under threat of contempt proceedings to testify.

B. Old Approach

1. A confession must be voluntarily made. If coerced, it will be inadmissible.

2. The Court did not have any definitive standard for lower courts to follow.

3. Based on case-by-case analysis. At first, coercion was deemed to include only physical and not mental intimidation.

4. Pre-*Miranda* cases:

Brown v. Mississippi, 297 U.S. 278 (1936)
Facts: The police took defendant to the crime scene and accused him of committing a crime. The defendant denied being involved. The police hung him from a tree. He was cut down and questioned again. He again denied guilt. He was then tied to a tree and whipped and he still denied guilt. He was freed. Later, the police again seized him and whipped him until he finally confessed.

Held: The Supreme Court held that the defendant's Fourteenth Amendment due process rights were violated. The Court noted defendant's confession resulted from brutality and coercion.

Chambers v. Florida, 309 U.S. 227 (1940)

Facts: The police arrested four teenagers for murder. The youths were questioned for many hours. They were held in jail without outside contact for long periods of time. The teenagers finally confessed.

Held: The Supreme Court reversed their convictions. The Court held that the confessions were "coerced" because of the long questioning sessions and the lack of outside contact. The confessions violated the teenagers' Fourteenth Amendment rights.

Ashcraft v. Tennessee, 322 U.S. 143 (1944)

Facts: The defendant was arrested for murder. He was questioned for two days straight, without sleep, until he finally confessed.

Held: The Court overturned his conviction. As in the prior case, it held that this type of questioning was "coercion" and therefore a violation of the defendant's Fourteenth Amendment rights.

Spano v. New York, 360 U.S. 315 (1959)

Facts: The defendant was a suspect in an ongoing murder investigation. The defendant called a friend who was on the police force and confessed that he shot the victim in self defense. The officer told his superiors. The defendant was brought in to the station house - his attorney told him to say nothing. After many hours of interrogation had failed to produce a confession, the friend/officer was called in to elicit a confession from his friend by preying on his sympathies toward the officer. The defendant did not cooperate at first, but on the fourth attempt told the police officer/friend about the shooting.

Held: The Court held that this type of psychological pressure is deceptive and against fundamental fairness. The Court also held that this type of questioning was in violation of the defendant's constitutional rights.

Massiah v. United States, 377 U.S. 201 (1964)
Held: Police may not question a suspect in the absence of counsel once that person has been *indicted or arraigned.* Use of any statement so obtained violates the accused's Sixth Amendment right to counsel.

Escobedo v. Illinois, 378 U.S. 748 (1964)
Facts: The defendant was arrested, brought down to a police station, and questioned. The defendant made repeated requests to see his attorney. The attorney, who was at the police station, also asked to see his client. The police denied all such requests. The defendant, under protracted interrogation, finally confessed

Held: The Supreme Court held that the defendant's Constitutional right to counsel had been violated. The Court noted that once an investigation turns from general fact finding to a particular suspect, and that suspect asks for counsel and counsel is not supplied, and the police have not warned the suspect to remain silent, then any confession during that investigation would be inadmissible. In such a case, the accused has been deprived the *assistance of counsel* in violation of the Sixth Amendment.

Note: This case created a pre-indictment right to counsel under the Sixth Amendment.

C.   **New Standard**

1. *Miranda v. Arizona*, 384 U.S. 436 (1966)
Facts: The defendant was arrested and charged with rape. The police questioned Miranda for a mere two hours, and he signed a written confession. Prosecutors used Miranda's confession to obtain a conviction.

Held: The prosecution may not use any statements stemming from "custodial interrogation" of a defendant unless it demonstrates the use of "*procedural safeguards*" effective to serve the privilege against self incrimination. *Custodial interrogation* means questioning initiated by law enforcement officers after:
  a) A person has been taken into custody, or
  b) A person has otherwise been deprived of his freedom in any significant way.

2. Procedural safeguards - A suspect must be:

  a. Informed of his right to remain silent;

  b. Told that anything he says may be used against him in a court of law;

  c. Informed that he has a right to the presence of an attorney, either retained or appointed;

  d. Apprised that if he cannot afford an attorney, that one will be provided to him.

  Most State constitutions add a fifth right: "You may terminate questioning at any time."

3. Rights may be Waived.

    a. Requirements
        (i) Burden of proof on prosecution;
        (ii) Intelligent and voluntary waiver of rights.

    b. Intelligent and Voluntary
        (i) Intelligent - suspect knows and appreciates what she is doing and is sufficiently competent to waive those rights.
        (ii) Not valid if suspect is drunk, too young, in a state of trauma, or seriously mentally ill. *But see Colorado v. Connelly, infra.*
        (iii) No definite guidelines - must be judged on a case-by-case basis.

    c. Silence never constitutes a waiver.

    d. Signed waiver not required but is extremely helpful in proving that waiver was intelligent and voluntary.

4. If a suspect indicates the desire to speak with an attorney at any time, there can be no questioning.

5. Likewise, if an individual is alone and indicates that she does not want to be interrogated, the police may not question her.

6. Failure to ask for a lawyer does not constitute waiver of the right to counsel.

    Policy: Custodial interrogations are *presumptively coercive* -- as such, they require procedural safeguards to protect a defendants constitutional right not to incriminate himself.

    Note: The Court says that warnings are required by the Constitution, but not necessarily theses warnings.

7. Confessions can still be challenged in the traditional way.

8. The meaning of "interrogation," "testimony" and "custody.

For *Miranda* to kick in, you must have:
  (a) Interrogation,
  (b) Testimony, and
  (c) Custody.

a. Interrogation

> **Rhode Island v. Innis**, 446 U.S. 291 (1980)
> **Rule**: *Interrogation* may be *express* or its *functional equivalent* --
> i.e., a practice that police should know is reasonably likely to
> evoke an incriminatory response from a suspect.
>
> **Note:** A police officer's*intent* in making a statement is not
> determinative in deciding whether a suspect has been interrogated,
> but may be an important factor to consider.
>
> **Facts:** Here, Innis was arrested on suspicion of murdering a taxi
> cab driver with a shotgun, though when arrested, Innis was not
> carrying a weapon. The police properly advised him of his
> *Miranda* rights. Innis indicated that he understood those rights and
> wanted to speak to an attorney. Innis was then placed in the back
> of a "caged wagon" -- a four door police car with wire screen mesh
> separating the front and rear seats. While the officers were
> specifically instructed not to engage Innis in conversation, they
> carried on a conversation of their own. The officers discussed how
> sad it would be if one of the little handicapped children from a
> local school discovered Innis' shotgun and killed herself. At that
> point, Innis interrupted the conversation, stating that he wanted to
> show the officers where the gun was located. Innis was read his
> *Miranda* rights again, and lead the police to the murder weapon.

Held: The police officers would not necessarily have known that their conversation would be "reasonably likely" to "evoke an incriminatory response" from Innis, and therefore, there was no "interrogation."

b. Testimony

Pennsylvania v. Muniz, 496 U.S. 582 (1990)
Rule: A person may be compelled to provide *evidence* against himself, but may not be compelled to give *testimony*.

Facts: Police asked Muniz a series of questions relating to his height, weight and date of birth, video taped him taking a sobriety test, and took his fingerprints in an effort to compile evidence to be used against him in a prosecution for drunk driving. No *Miranda* warnings were given.

Held: The "physical inability to articulate words in a clear manner" is *physical evidence* and not "testimony," and therefore, may be used against the defendant. The Court split, however, on the admissibility of Muniz's answer to one of the questions posed by the police -- "Do you know what the date was of your sixth birthday?" A majority of the Court agreed that asking this question subjected Muniz to the "cruel trilemma" of truth, falsity or silence, and Muniz's answer to the question, "I don't know," was held not to be admissible in the absence of *Miranda* warnings.

Note: This case highlights the distinction between physical evidence and testimony. Slurred speech, for example, evidences a defendant's physical condition, but does not encompass testimony. As evidenced by the birthday question, the line between what is mere physical evidence of a defendant's condition and what is testimonial is not always clear.

c.   Custody

(i)   A suspect is *in custody* when he has been arrested, or when his freedom has been limited in a significant way.
E.g., a suspect is taken down to police station and subjected to questioning.

(ii) An ordinary traffic stop is "non-threatening" and does not `constitute *custody* for *Miranda* purposes.

(iii) *Terry* stops are not generally subject to *Miranda* warnings -- suspects are not "in custody."

Note: Police need to be able to make on-the-street inquiries to carry out investigative functions. Once police suspicion ripens, a suspect must be read his rights.

(iv) Unless a probation officer threatens to violate a probationer's probation, the probationer, even though subject to testimonial interrogation at the officer's house, is not *in custody*, and therefore, need not be given *Miranda* warnings.

9. Invocations of the right to silence or counsel

a.   An invocation of the *right to silence* must be "scrupulously honored," though with the passage of sufficient time, the police may reapproach a suspect and resume questioning.

b.   Invocations of the right to counsel

Edwards v. Arizona, 451 U.S. 477 (1981)
Rule: An accused, having invoked the right to counsel, is not subject to further interrogation by the authorities until counsel has been made available to him, unless:
1.   The accused, himself, *initiates* further communication, exchanges or conversations with the police, *and*
2.   The accused makes a knowing and intelligent waiver of the right to counsel under the totality of the circumstances -- the prosecution bears the burden of proof.

(i) Meaning of "initiate"

> ***Oregon v. Bradshaw***, 462 U.S. 1039 (1983)
> **Facts:** Bradshaw had invoked the right to counsel.
> While being transported to a detention facility, he
> asked "what is going to happen to me now?"
>
> **Held:** Bradshaw had "initiated" a conversation with
> the police.
>
> **Note:** In reality, Bradshaw probably just wanted to
> know where he was being taken to -- Chief Justice
> Rehnquist and a majority of the Court, however,
> agreed that Bradshaw, by his statement, had "initiated"
> a conversation with the police and waived his right to
> counsel.

(ii) Meaning of "invoke"

> **Rule:** Unless an invocation of the right to counsel is
> reasonably clear, the right does not accrue. *See Davis
> v. United States,* 512 U.S. 452 (1944).
>
> **Net:** Unless a suspect says, "I want an attorney," or
> makes a similar reasonably clear invocation of her
> right to counsel, police are not required to do anything:
> (1) They need not clarify whether the suspect was, in
> fact, attempting to assert her right to counsel; and
> (2) They may continue interrogating the suspect.

c. Once a defendant claims the Fifth Amendment right to counsel,
police may not talk to him outside the presence of counsel until all
appeals are exhausted.

> (1) In *Arizona v. Roberson,* 486 U.S. 675 (1988), the
> Court held that once a defendant invokes his right to

counsel on one crime, he may not be questioned by police outside the presence of counsel about other crimes (unless, of course, he "initiates" a conversation with police within the meaning of *Edwards* and *Bradshaw*).

(2) In *Minnick v. Mississippi,* 498 U.S. 146 (1990), the Court held that police may not question a suspect who has invoked the right to counsel *after* he has consulted with, but outside the presence of, counsel.

Net: Together, *Roberson* and *Minnick* make clear that once a suspect invokes her Fifth Amendment right to counsel, police may not question the suspect in the absence of counsel, even about separate offenses and even if new warnings are given by the police.

10. Police trickery, warnings and waiver

a. Undercover agent cases

Illinois v. Perkins, 496 U.S. 292 (1990)
Facts: Police inserted an undercover agent ("UA") into Perkins jail cell. Without issuing a *Miranda* warning, the UA engaged Perkins in conversation and questioned him about a crime for which he was not arrested or indicted (thus, the Sixth Amendment was not implicated). *See Brewer, Henry, Jackson, infra, and Massiah supra.*

Held: Statements made by Perkins to the UA were admissible, even though no *Miranda* warnings were given.

Policy: In the atmosphere of the jail cell, the station-house dangers of blue uniforms and police coercion are not present. Coercion is the primary danger against which the *Miranda* Court sought to protect.

Note: This holding is limited to UA (undercover agent) cases.

Moran v. Burbine, 475 U.S. 412 (1986)
Facts: While Burbine was in police custody, his sister obtained a lawyer to represent him. The lawyer phoned the police station and "received assurances" that Burbine would not be questioned until the next day. Notwithstanding the assurances made to counsel, the police engaged in an interrogation of Burbine later that same day that yielded inculpatory statements that were used to convict Burbine. Before the interrogation session, Burbine was informed of his rights under *Miranda*, and executed a series of voluntary waivers of those rights. He then confessed to the murder of a young woman.

Held: Burbine understood his rights and validly waived them. Justice O'Connor, writing for the majority, reasoned that "[e]vents occurring outside of the presence of the suspect and entirely unknown to him surely can have no bearing on the capacity to comprehend and knowingly relinquish a constitutional right" and that "the state of mind of the police is irrelevant to the question of the intelligence and voluntariness of respondent's election to abandon his rights." Justice O'Connor declined to read *Miranda* as forbidding deliberate police deception of an attorney, and refused to require the police to inform a suspect of his attorney's efforts to reach him.

Note: *Moran* and *Bourbine* turn on the modern Court's reading of *Miranda* -- that the real purpose of *Miranda* was to put an end to **physical** coercion. These defendants were not pressured or coerced into giving testimony, but merely tricked.

11.   Erosion of Miranda -- A return to voluntariness

a.   There is a *public safety* exception to the requirement that *Miranda* warnings be given before a suspect's answers may be admitted into evidence, and the availability of that exception does not depend upon the motivation of the individual officers involved.

New York v. Quarles, 467 U.S. 649 (1984)
Facts: Two officers, Kraft and Scarring, were on patrol when they were approached by a woman who told them that she had just been

raped by a six foot tall black man wearing a black jacket with the name "Big Ben" printed in yellow letters on the back. She also told the officers that the man, who was carrying a gun, had just entered an A & P supermarket located nearby. Officer Kraft entered the supermarket and soon spotted Quarles who matched the description given. At the same time, Quarles spotted Officer Kraft, turned around, and fled down an aisle. Kraft gave chase with gun drawn, but lost sight of Quarles for a few moments before regaining sight of him and ordering Quarles to stop, which he did. By that time, three other officers had arrived on the scene. Officer Kraft frisked Quarles and found that he was wearing an empty shoulder holster. After handcuffing him, and before issuing any *Miranda* warnings, Kraft asked Quarles where the gun was. Quarles nodded in the direction of some empty cartons nearby. Officer Kraft retrieved a .38 caliber pistol and then read Quarles his *Miranda* rights.

Held: "The need for answers to questions in a situation posing a threat to the public safety outweighs the need for the prophylactic rule protecting the Fifth Amendment's privilege against self-incrimination." Thus, the Court held that the gun need not be suppressed. As long as the gun remained concealed in the supermarket, it posed a number of dangers to the public -- the Court reasoned that an accomplice might use it, or a customer or store employee might later find it.

Policy: The Court did not want police officers to have to chose between asking questions without *Miranda* warnings, rendering whatever evidence they may come upon inadmissible, or issuing *Miranda* warnings and possibly destroying their ability to obtain dangerous physical evidence.

Note: Not many courts have adopted the public safety exception, though it would seem that many police questions regarding the location of drugs and weapons could be justified on the basis of public safety.

b. The Court adjusts the "fruits" doctrine

Michigan v. Tucker, 417 U.S. 433 (1974)
Facts: Police questioned Tucker without informing him that he had the right to appointed counsel if he was indigent. Tucker told the police that he was with a friend at the time that the crime for which he was under investigation was committed. Upon being questioned by the police, however, the friend made statements which implicated Tucker in the crime.

Held: Testimony of a third party witness acquired by police as a direct result of police failure to give a suspect full *Miranda* warnings does not render the testimony inadmissible under the Exclusionary Rule as the fruit of a poisonous tree.

Oregon v. Elstad, 470 U.S. 298 (1985)
Rule: Despite the absence of *Miranda* warnings in the first instance, which produces an incriminating statement, a subsequent confession following a waiver of a defendant's *Miranda* rights is not excludible as the fruit of a poisonous tree (the poisonous tree, of course, being the first illegally obtained confession).

Facts: Police investigating a burglary suspected Elstad, an 18 year old neighbor of the home that was burglarized. The police executed an arrest warrant at Elstad's home, and proceeded to question Elstad about the burglary. Elstad quickly confessed, and he was brought down to the police station where, an hour later, he was given *Miranda* warnings. Elstad then gave a full statement which was typed, read back to him and initialed. The statement was used to help convict Elstad at his burglary trial.

Held: The fruit of the poisonous tree doctrine does not apply with the same force to a *Miranda* violation. The Court opted for a voluntariness test (for the second-in-time confession), stating that "there is no warrant for presuming coercive effect where the suspect's initial inculpatory statement, though technically in violation of *Miranda*, was voluntary."

Implications of *Elstad*: If the police do not give *Miranda* warnings, they can take a pot luck crack at interrogating a suspect. If the suspect confesses, he will be much more likely later to waive his *Miranda* rights because he thinks that the "cat is [already] out of the bag." Thus, *Elstad* encourages police to take chances. It is an open invitation to avoid *Miranda*.

c.   Focus is on coercive police activity

Colorado v. Connelly, 479 U.S. 157 (1986)
Facts: Connelly approached a police officer in downtown Denver, stated that he had "killed a girl last year," and that he wanted to talk about it. The officer informed Connelly of his rights to remain silent and to counsel, but Connelly insisted that he wanted to talk about it. A homicide detective arrived upon the scene and repeated the *Miranda* warnings. At that point, Connelly stated that he had flown from Boston to confess the murder of a young girl he had murdered in Denver months ago. Connelly was taken to the police station where he discussed the details of the murder with the police. The next morning, Connelly became disoriented -- he claimed that the "voice of God" told him to confess. Connelly was initially found incompetent to participate in his own defense, and an expert witness at his trial found him to be suffering from schizophrenia.

Held: A mentally ill person can make a knowing and intelligent waiver of his *Miranda* rights. Police have the burden of proof to prove waiver by a preponderance of the evidence. Chief Justice Rhenquist, writing for a majority of the Court, stated that "coercive police activity is a necessary predicate to the finding that a confession is not voluntary within the meaning of the Due Process clause of the Fourteenth Amendment." Here, the police did nothing coercive -- there was no improper state action.

Note: The modern Court's case-by-case inquiry into voluntariness is gradually chipping away at *Miranda's* presumption of coercion and involuntariness.

d. Further erosion of Miranda

1. Statements made by a defendant, though inadmissible because police failed to give proper *Miranda* warnings, may be used to impeach a defendant's testimony so long as the statements were not the result of police coercion. *See Harris v. New York*, 401 U.S. 222 (1971).

2. A waiver of *Miranda* rights is not invalid simply because the police fail to inform a suspect of every crime they suspect him of committing. *See Colorado v. Spring*, 479 U.S. 564 (1987).

IX. Right to Counsel

The Sixth Amendment states in part "...in all criminal prosecutions, the accused shall enjoy the right ... to have Assistance of Counsel for his defense." The right to counsel is fundamental to our system of justice to ensure the fundamental human rights of life and liberty.

A. Theory

> *Scottsboro Cases* - *Powell v. Alabama*, 287 U.S. 45 (1932); *Johnson v. Zerbrest*, 304 U.S. 458 (1938).
> **Holdings**: An accused is entitled to the assistance of counsel from the time of arraignment, and Courts indulge in every reasonable presumption against waiver of fundamental constitutional rights, such as the right to the assistance of counsel.

B. Obtaining Counsel

1. Court Appointed Counsel
    a. If a person cannot afford an attorney - one will be appointed for them at the first critical stage of prosecution (usually preliminary hearing).

    b. The court appointed attorney may be a public defender or a private attorney.

    c. An indigent person has no say in who the appointed attorney is. Though he may, upon good cause, seek the attorney's dismissal.

2. Privately Retained Counsel
   a. Chosen by client.

   b. At anytime during the prosecution of a case.

   c. Choice of counsel is limited only to the extent that ethical
      rules governing attorney conduct so provide.
      E.g., an attorney cannot take on a case if to do so would create
      a conflict of interest.

C. **The Sixth Amendment Right to Counsel Revisited**

Rule: "Once adversary proceedings have commenced against an
individual, he has a right to representation when the government
interrogates him."

Brewer v. Williams, 430 U.S. 387 (1977)
Facts: On Christmas Eve in 1968, 10 year old Pamela Powers had
been watching her brother's wrestling match at the Des Moines, Iowa
YMCA when she went to the wash room -- she was never again seen
by her family alive. Williams, an escaped mental patient, was seen
leaving the YMCA carrying a bundle of clothing with two pale, white
legs sticking out of it, and placing the bundle in his car. Two days
later, Williams turned himself in, on the advice of his Des Moines
counsel, to the Davenport police, 160 miles east of Des Moines.
Williams was informed of his *Miranda* rights, and instructed by his
Davenport attorney not to speak to the police until after he had spoken
to his Des Moines attorney. The police were instructed not to question
or mistreat Williams while transporting him back to Des Moines. In
the meantime, Williams was arraigned before a judge in Davenport. At
no time during the 160 mile trip did Williams express a willingness to
be questioned. En route to Des Moines, Detective Leaming delivered the
infamous "Christian burial speech." He told Williams, among other
things, that a snow storm was coming, and that Williams was the only
person who knew where the little girl's body was; that once snow was
on top of it, Williams, himself, might not be able to locate the body;

that they would be traveling right past the body anyway; and that "this little girl should be entitled to a Christian burial for the little girl who was snatched away on Christmas Eve and murdered." Williams ultimately lead detective Leaming to Pamela Power's body.

Held: Williams was entitled to the assistance of counsel guaranteed to him by the Sixth and Fourteenth Amendments, and therefore, his statements and actions, made outside of the presence of counsel and leading the police to the body of Pamela Powers, could not be used against him.

Note: The term "interrogation" is not apt in Sixth Amendment cases. Instead, the focus is on the *intent* of the officer -- did the police engage in a post-indictment, or post-arraignment attempt to *deliberately elicit* testimony outside the presence of counsel? Any such elicitation is in violation of a defendant's Sixth Amendment right to legal representation. Here, because the police attempted to *deliberately elicit* such testimony, after the Sixth Amendment right to counsel had attached, William's statements were inadmissible.

1. Jail cell informant cases

Rule: Once formal proceedings have begun, *Massiah* dictates that the government may not "*deliberately elicit*" information from a suspect without first obtaining a knowing and voluntary waiver of the suspect's Sixth Amendment rights.

United States v. Henry, 447 U.S. 264 (1980)
Facts: Following Henry's Arraignment, the police placed a paid informant in Henry's cell. The informant was told not to initiate any conversations with Henry but to be alert and to listen to anything Henry said about the armed bank robbery he was suspected of committing.

Held: "By intentionally creating a situation likely to induce Henry to make incriminating statements without the assistance of counsel, the government violated Henry's Sixth Amendment right to counsel."

Important Factors: Here, the Court found that the following factors compelled a finding of *deliberate elicitation* by the government:
    (a) The police conduct was *deliberate*,
    (b) The defendant was in custody, and
    (c) The informant posed as an inmate.

Kuhlman v. Wilson, 477 U.S. 436 (1986)
Facts: Lee, an inmate, was placed in Kuhlmann's cell prior to his arrival to act as an informant. Lee was instructed not to "actively question" Kuhlmann about the crimes with which Kuhlmann was charged. At first Kuhlmann told Lee that he was present at the robbery but did not know the robbers. Lee responded that Kuhlmann's story "didn't sound too good." Kuhlmann ultimately confessed to Lee to having participated in the robbery and murder.

Held: Distinguishing *Henry*, the Court held that the Sixth Amendment was not violated as the informant made no effort to "stimulate" conversations about the crimes charged.

Note: If you are having difficulty distinguishing *Henry* from *Kuhlmann* on its facts, you are in good company. Three Justices of the Supreme Court, Brennan, Marshall and Stevens, found the cases to be virtually indistinguishable.

Net: The threshold inquiry in any post-indictment informant case is is the government engaged in active solicitation, or is the informant merely a passive listener. These cases could go either way.

2. **The Sixth Amendment right to counsel is "offense-specific"** -- it does not protect a suspect *vis a vis* other crimes.

While *Massiah* and *Henry* apply to the crime that is under indictment, they do not protect a defendant from disclosing information concerning *other crimes* -- police can send in an informant to gather evidence of other crimes, just not of the crimes charged in the indictment.

    a.   E.g., **D** invoked her Sixth Amendment right to counsel with regard to **crime A**. Police approach **D** and question her on **crime B**. **D** waives her *Miranda* rights and confesses to the much more serious **crime B**. **D** says "*Roberson!*" -- having invoked my Sixth Amendment right to counsel on **crime A**, you cannot question me on other crimes. The Court has held that "incriminating statements pertaining to other crimes, as to which the Sixth Amendment right to counsel has not yet attached, are, of course, admissible at a trial of those offenses." *McNeil v. Wisconsin, 501 U.S. 171 (1991)*

3. If a defendant invokes his Sixth Amendment right to counsel when being arraigned, the police may not attempt to secure a waiver from him unless he *initiates* a conversation with them. *Michigan v. Jackson*, 475 U.S. 625 (1986).

Note: Most defendants will request counsel when asked by the arraignment judge if they would like counsel.

D. Eyewitness Identification

1. The Right to Counsel at Lineups, Showups and Photographic Arrays

   a. Lineups

   United States v. Wade, 388 U.S. 218 (1967)
   Facts: Wade was indicted and later arrested for his part in a bank robbery. Fifteen days after counsel was appointed to represent him, an FBI agent, without notice to Wade's lawyer, arranged to have bank employee witnesses view a lineup made up of Wade and five or six other prisoners. Both witnesses identified Wade as the robber. Wade was identified by the witnesses in court at Wade's trial, and evidence of the earlier lineup identifications came in on cross-examination.

   Held: The Sixth Amendment right to counsel attaches at the "critical stages" of a criminal prosecution. Because a lineup identification is such a "critical stage," any lineup identification procedure conducted in the absence of counsel is not admissible at trial. If a witness, based on a number of factors, can convince a court that she had an independent basis for her in-court identification, then that identification evidence is admissible.

   Note: The *Wade* Court found that the following factors can provide a basis for a determination whether a given witness had an independent source for an in-court identification:
   (i)   Prior opportunity to observe,
   (ii) Discrepancy between pre-lineup description and defendant's actual appearance.
   (iii) Whether the witness identified someone other than the defendant,
   (iv) Opportunity to view during commission of crime, and
   (v)   Failure to identify defendant on prior occasion.

b. Showups

    Kirby v. Illinois, 406 U.S. 682 (1972)
    Held: The *Wade per se* exclusionary rule does not apply to
    identification testimony based upon a police station showup that
    takes place *before* the defendant has been indicted or otherwise
    formally charged with any offense.

    Note: There are virtually no post-indictment lineups in the real
    world.

c. Photographic identifications

    United States v. Ash, 413 U.S. 300 (1973)
    Held: A post-indictment photographic identification is not a "critical
    stage" of a criminal adversary proceeding, and therefore, there is no
    Sixth Amendment right to have counsel present at a post-indictment
    photographic identification procedure.

    Rationale: In a photographic identification, the defendant is not
    present, and therefore, there is no confrontation between the defendant
    and the machinery of the state, thus, the defendant has no right to
    have counsel present. Also, photographic identifications are part of
    the routine police investigatory process, outside the traditional role of
    counsel.

E.   The Due Process approach

1.   The Due Process clause protects against *unfair* and *unduly suggestive* identification procedures -- acts as a backup to *Wade* and *Kirby*.

Stovall v. Denno, 388 U.S. 293 (1967)
Facts: Stovall was arrested for stabbing Dr. Paul Behrendt to death and stabbing his wife, also a physician, 11 times. On the day following the attack while Mrs. Behrendt was hospitalized, the police brought Stovall, handcuffed to a police officer and the only African American in the group, into Mrs. Behrendt's hospital room where she positively identified him as the person who attacked her and killed her husband. She also made an in court identification of Stovall during his trial.

Held: It must be determined under a *totality of the circumstances* whether an out-of-court identification procedure was *unnecessarily suggestive.*

1.   Evidence obtained by use of an unduly suggestive identification procedure is inadmissible, unless there was an *exigency* which justified a confrontation on less than optimal circumstances. Here, there was such an exigency -- no one knew how long Mrs. Behrendt might live -- only her words could have exonerated Stovall. Thus, the showup identification procedure was necessary under a totality of the circumstances.

2.   If the Court finds the out-of-court identification procedure to have been unnecessarily suggestive, the in court identification is admissible if the Court finds that there was an independent source for the identification.

Simmons v. United States, 390 U.S. 377 (1968)
Held: *Stovall totality of the circumstances* test applies to photographic identification procedures.

Test: Whether a given "photographic identification procedure was so impermissibly suggestive as to give rise to a very substantial likelihood of irreparable misidentification?"

2. A shift towards reliability

a. In ***Neil v. Biggers***, 409 U.S. 188 (1972), the Court held that the *reliability* of an out-of-court identification procedure is the linchpin. *Reliability* of a witness' identification could sanitize both in court and out-of-court identification procedures. Justice Powell, writing for the majority, did not factor the suggestiveness of the identification procedure into the calculus.

3. The modern approach

Manson v. Brathwaite, 432 U.S. 98 (1977)
Facts: A police officer was shown a single photograph of the defendant two days after he engaged the defendant in an undercover drug buy. The photograph was admitted into evidence at the defendant's trial and the officer made an in court identification.

Held: "[R]eliability is the linchpin in determining the admissibility of identification testimony for both pre- and post-*Stovall* confrontations. The factors to be considered ... include the opportunity to view the criminal at the time of the crime, the witness' degree of attention, the accuracy of his prior description of the criminal, the level of certainty demonstrated at the confrontation, and the time between the crime and the confrontation. Against these factors is to be weighed the corrupting effect of the suggestive identification itself."

Note: The test under *Manson* is basically the same for in court and out-of-court identification procedures, whereas under *Stovall*, any *suggestive* out-of-court identification would be banned, *per se*, from evidence, without regard to its reliability.

F.   Right to Counsel at Trial

1. *See Gideon v. Wainwright*, 372 U.S. 335 (1963) (extending the Sixth Amendment right to counsel to the states).

2. *Argersinger v. Hamlin*, 407 U.S. 25 (1972) (absent knowing and intelligent waiver of the right to counsel, no person may be imprisoned for *any* offense, whether classified as petty, misdemeanor or felony, unless he was represented by counsel at his trial).

G.   Ineffective Assistance of Counsel.

1. Very hard to prove.

2. A convicted defendant's claim that counsel's assistance was so defective as to require the reversal of a conviction has two components:
    a. A defendant must establish that counsel's performance was *so deficient* that counsel was not functioning as "counsel" guaranteed by the Sixth Amendment; and
    b. The defendant must show that the deficient performance *prejudiced* the defense; i.e., that counsel's errors were so serious as to deprive the defendant of a fair trial.

3. *See Strickland v. Washington*, 466 U.S. 668 (1984) (result would be different if inadequate performance of counsel did not occur).

4. Must show that counsel made serious errors which prejudiced the defense.

5. A knowing and voluntary guilty plea waives all appeals based upon ineffective assistance of counsel.

H.   *Pro Se* **Representation**

Sadly, many people lack the resources necessary to obtain counsel to protect their fundamental rights to life and liberty.

1. A defendant may choose to represent himself.

2. Constitutional requirements before a judge will allow representation *pro se*:
    a. Accused must be made aware of her right to counsel;

    b. Accused must expressly waive that right;

    c. The accused must be competent to make such a waiver to represent herself.

X. Other Constitutional Rights

The Bill of Rights to our Constitution guarantees the accused many rights. This chapter explores important highly accepted and followed rights all pertaining to the trial stage of a criminal proceeding.

A.   **Trial by Jury**

1.   Article III, Section 2, Clause 3. Does not require a set number of jurors.

2.   The Fourteenth Amendment guarantees the right to trial by jury in all criminal cases.

3.   Federal statute mandates 12 jurors on any criminal prosecution.

4.   Minimum number of jurors allowed in state criminal prosecution is six unless prosecution is capital in nature. *See Williams v. Florida*, 399 U.S. 78 (1970) (twelve person jury not required ingredient of trial by jury).

5.   Unanimous verdicts
     a.   Unanimity is one of the indispensable features of a federal jury trial. *See Andres v. United States*, 333 U.S. 740 (1948); *Patton v. United States*, 281 U.S. 281 U.S. 276 (1930); *Hawaii v. Makerlin*, 190 U.S. 197, 211-12 (1903).

     b.   Lower standard allowed for state criminal trials. Under provisions of State law authorizing a guilty verdict or acquittal by nine of the twelve jurors in a criminal case in which punishment is hard labor, conviction is not in violation of Sixth Amendment right to trial by jury. However, a unanimous verdict is required in capital cases. *See Johnson v. Louisiana*, 406 US 356 (1972). *See also Apodaca v. Oregon*, 406 U.S. 404 (1972).

     Note: Whether the Court would uphold conviction on less than nine votes is yet to be seen.

6. Only in serious offenses.

    a. No offense can be deemed "petty" for purposes of the right to trial by jury where imprisonment for more than six months is authorized. *See Baldwin v. New York*, 399 U.S. 66 (1970).

    b. If *possible penalty* is six months or less, then no right to trial by jury.

7. Trial by jury in the juvenile courts is not a constitutional requirement, though many states require the use of juries in juvenile court proceedings. *McKeiver v. Pennsylvania*, 403 U.S. 528 (1971).

8. Right may be waived:
    a. Only upon express *consent* of prosecutor and court. *See Singer v. United States*, 380 U.S. 24 (1965).

    b. Intelligent.

9. *Voir Dire* (Jury Selection)
    a. Challenges to eliminate jury members.
        (i) Each party to a criminal proceeding has the right to make a limited number of *peremptory challenges*. These challenges may usually be made for any *reason* at all, as long as that *reason* is related to a party's view concerning the outcome of the case to be tried. *See infra Batson v. Kentucky*, 476 U.S. 79, 89 (1986). Each side gets a limited number of these.
        (ii) For Cause - challenges which state a reason why a juror must be stricken from the *venire*. These are unlimited in number.

    b. The equal protection clause however, forbids a prosecutor from challenging potential jurors solely on account of their race. *Id.*

Batson v. Kentucky, 476 U.S. 79 (1986)
Facts: During the trial of a black man in Kentucky, the trial judge allowed the prosecutor to exercise his peremptory challenges to strike all four black persons on the *venire*, and an all-white jury was selected which ultimately convicted the defendant.

Held: A state denies a black defendant the equal protection of the laws when it places him on trial before a jury from which members of his race have been purposefully excluded. To establish a *prima facia* case of purposeful discrimination, a defendant must show: (1) that he is a member of a cognizable racial group, (2) that the prosecutor has exercised peremptory challenges to remove members of the defendant's racial group, and (3) that facts and circumstances raise an inference that peremptory challenges were used to exclude *venire* persons from the jury on account of their race. Once the defendant makes a *prima facia* showing, the burden shifts to the State to come forward with a neutral explanation for challenging black jurors.

B.   **Fair and Impartial Trial**

1. Circumstances surrounding a trial must not unduly influence jurors, though jurors need not be totally ignorant of the facts and issues involved in the trial.

2. Prejudicial publicity prohibited
   a. Change of Venue - if the trial atmosphere is "utterly corrupted by press coverage," the accused may have the trial moved to another jurisdiction where an impartial jury may be found. *See Murphy v. Florida*, 421 U.S. 794 (1975).

   b. Continuance - A Court may delay the start of a trial until a time when the trial is no longer a matter of public interest and an impartial jury may be chosen.

   c. Sequestration - Isolating jurors from the outside world and restricting juror contact with outsiders or news media so as to prevent the jury from being tainted by publicity.

   d. In order to guaranty a fair and impartial trial a court may:
      (i) Order all participants, including counsel and law enforcement personal, not to speak to the press or release any information to the public. This is known as a "gag order."
      (ii) Close proceedings to the press upon a showing that "closure is essential to preserve high values and is narrowly tailored to serve that interest." *See Press Enterprise Company v. Superior Court of California*, 478 U.S. 1, 13-14 (1986) In general, there is a qualified First Amendment right of access to criminal proceedings that applies to most preliminary hearings. The qualified First Amendment right of access can only be overcome if the *Press Enterprise* showing is made.
   Note: The First Amendment right of access to criminal proceedings cannot be overcome by conclusory assertions that publicly might deprive a defendant of the right to a fair and impartial trial.

C.   **Speedy and Public Trial**

1. All criminal defendants have the right to a speedy trial.

2. Speedy means that the trial is free from unnecessary or undue delay.

3. It is impossible to determine precisely when the right to a speedy trial has been denied. *See Barker v. Wingo*, 407 U.S. 514 (1972).

4. Factors to be considered:
    a. Length of delay;
    b. Reason for delay;
    c. Prejudice to the accused.

5. Public trial
    a. The right to a public trial is guaranteed to an accused. *See In re Oliver*, 333 U.S. 257 (1948).

    b. There is no corresponding right to a private trial.

    c. Upon good cause the court may exclude unruly spectators or limit the number of spectators. However, the judge cannot eliminate all family or friends of the accused from attending the trial. *See Garnett v. DePasquale*, 443 U.S. 368 (1979)

    c. Juveniles, unless charged and tried as adults, have no right to a public trial.

Easy Review for Criminal Procedure

D. **Right to Obtain Witnesses**

1. Defendants in criminal proceedings have a Sixth Amendment right to have compulsory process for obtaining witnesses.

2. This right includes:
   a. The power to subpoena witnesses;

   b. The right to present a defense;

   c. The right to present such persons to prove the defendant's version of the facts. *See Washington v. Texas*, 388 U.S. 14 (1967).

3. The right to compel the presence of witnesses generally does not extend beyond the territorial boundaries of the United States.

4. The government lacks the power to compel the presence at trial of foreign nationals residing outside of the United States.

5. The Defendant's inability to subpoena foreign witnesses is not a bar to a criminal prosecution.

E. **Right to Confront Witnesses**

1. A defendant must have an opportunity to conduct a meaningful cross-examination of the witnesses presented against her.

2. A defendant is "guaranteed the right to be present at any stage of the criminal procedure that is critical to its outcome if his presence would contribute to the fairness of the procedure." *See Kentucky v. Stincer*, 482 U.S. 730 (1987). For instance, a defendant generally has the right

to be present in court while adverse testimony is being given against him.

3. The right to be present is not absolute. A defendant's right to confront witnesses is not violated where the defendant:

    a. Is deliberately absent;

    b. Disrupts the courtroom.
        Court may (1) hold the defendant in contempt, (2) remove the defendant from the courtroom until he behaves.

4. An accused has the right to know who the prosecution's witnesses are:
    a. Name;

    b. Address;

    c. This right may be limited in circumstances where the witness' life may be in danger from revelation of that information.

5. Right to face witnesses

    a. In court.

    b. Face-to-face.

    c. Not by closed circuit television or through a semitransparent screen. *See Coy v. Iowa*, 487 U.S. 1012 (1988).

    d. However, right to confront witness is limited in child sex abuse and rape cases.

6. Child sex abuse cases.

Maryland v. Craig, 497 U.S. 836 (1990)
Held: The defendant's right to confront may be limited in cases of child sex abuse. Confrontation clause claims in child sex abuse cases must be evaluated on a case by case basis. Child witnesses may be able to testify outside of the presence of accused sex offenders, where *necessary*, by closed circuit television.

F.   **Double Jeopardy**

  1. Scope

      a. The Double Jeopardy clause prevents both successive punishments and successive prosecutions. *See, e.g., United States v. Ursery*, 518 U.S. 267 (1996).

         (i) An accused may not be *punished* for a crime in a criminal proceeding and later be punished again for the same offense.

         (ii) An accused may only be subjected to *one prosecution* for the same offense. *See, e.g., Witte v. United States*, 515 U.S. 389 (1995).

      b. An accused may be retried following a mistrial.

      c. Civil forfeitures do not impose "punishment" within the meaning of the Double Jeopardy clause. *See United States v. Ursery, supra.*

      d. An accused who successfully appeals a judgment of conviction on any ground other than insufficiency of the evidence may be re-prosecuted on the same charge. *See United States v. Scott*, 437 U.S. 82 (1978).

  2. Lesser included offenses

      a. An accused who is acquitted of a crime may not later be prosecuted for a lesser included offense of that crime.

         (i) For example, an accused who is acquitted of murder charges may not later be tried for manslaughter arising from the same set of facts involved in the murder prosecution.

         (ii) The state or federal government may, however, charge a defendant with both murder and manslaughter at the same time in a single prosecution.

G. Right to Proof Beyond a Reasonable Doubt

1. The prosecution bears the burden of proving each and every element of the offense charged, and must persuade the fact finder beyond a reasonable doubt of the accused's guilt.

   a. This requirement applies in state as well as federal criminal proceedings.

   b. The jury verdict required by the Sixth Amendment is a verdict of guilty beyond a reasonable doubt.

2. Reasonable Doubt
   Definition: "It is such a doubt as would cause a juror, after careful and candid and impartial consideration of all the evidence, to be so undecided that he cannot say that he has an abiding conviction of the defendant's guilt. It is such a doubt as would cause a reasonable person to hesitate or pause in the graver or more important transactions of life. However, it is not a fanciful doubt, not a whimsical doubt, nor a doubt based on conjecture. It is a doubt, which I say, is based on reason. The government is not required to establish guilt beyond all doubt, or to a mathematical certainty or a scientific certainty. Its burden is to establish guilt beyond a reasonable doubt,." Excerpt from *Moore v. U.S.*, 345 F.2d 97 (D.C. Cir. 1965).

XI. Special Defenses

A.   **Insanity Defense**

Four Types of Insanity Tests

1. M'Naghten Test

2. Irresistible Impulse Test

3. Model Penal Code Test

4. Durham/Product Test

1. M'Naghten Test
   a. Widely used today by the courts.

   b. Criminal liability will be excused if the criminal act occurred as a result of mental illness such that the "accused did not know the nature or quality of his acts; or if he did not know that what he was doing was wrong."

2. Irresistible Impulse Test
   a. Criminal liability is excused if "the accused did not have the ability to control his conduct even if he knew that what he was doing was wrong."

   b. Loss of control by voluntary intoxication is no defense.

   c. The "irresistible impulse" test is recognized by a minority of jurisdictions and may be used as a supplement to the M'Naghten test. *M'Naghten's Case*, 10 cl. & fin.200, 8 Eng. Rep. (1843).

3. Model Penal Code

    a. Criminal liability is excused if it is shown that the accused suffers from a mental disease or defect and that the accused "lacked substantial capacity either to appreciate the wrongfulness of his or her conduct or to conform his or her conduct to the requirements of the law."

    b. Also widely used by courts.

    c. Unlike the M'Naghten test, the Model Penal Code test does not require the accused to lack complete knowledge that the act was wrong.

4. Durham/Product Test

    a. Excludes from punishment criminal conduct that was "the product of a mental disease or defect." *See Durham v. United States*, 214 F.2d 862 (1954).

    b. Very liberal and broad standard.

5. In the vast majority of states, the accused carries the burden of proof on the issue of insanity.

B.   Entrapment
1. The focus is on the predisposition of a defendant to commit the crime with which he or she has been charged.

2. In order to find that a defendant has been "entrapped," a court must find that absent government inducement, the accused would never have committed the crime charged. In the words of Justice Rhenquist, "only when the government's deception actually implants the criminal design

in the mind of the defendant" does the defense of entrapment come into play. *Hampton v. United States*, 425 U.S. 484 (1976).

    a. Courts look at the accused's past criminal history and "tendencies."

    b. This approach is favored by Chief Justice Rehnquist, but a majority of the court has never held that "an analysis other than one limited to predisposition would never be appropriate under due process principles." *Hampton*, 425 U.S. at 493 (Powell, J., concurring).

In ***United States v. Russell***, 411 U.S. 423 (1973) The Court set forth the subjective "predisposition" test, but also stated that, "we may some day be presented with a situation in which the conduct of law enforcement agents is so outrageous that due process principles would absolutely bar the government from involving judicial processes to obtain a conviction."

Note: Under present law, courts apply the predisposition test, but where the conduct of law enforcement agents is particularly outrageous, courts may look to objective standards of fairness and due process. Indeed, Russell has been cited by over 200 courts as authority for an entrapment defense based solely on an objective assessment of the government's conduct.

3. Objective Test

a. Accused's past "predisposition" is irrelevant because the focus is on the government's actions.

b. The focus is on the conduct of the government agent - could activities of the government agent have induced an innocent party to commit a crime?

c. An accused may challenge the prosecution's case against him or her and plead entrapment at the same time.

Text of Amendments I through XVI of the Untied States Constitution

Amendment I.

Congress shall make no law respecting an establishment of religion, or prohibiting the free exercise thereof; or abridging the freedom of speech, or of the press, or the right of the people peaceably to assemble, and to petition the Government for a redress of grievances.

Amendment II.

A well regulated Militia, being necessary to the security of a free State, the right of the people to keep and bear Arms, shall not be infringed.

Amendment III.

No Soldier shall, in time of peace be quartered in any house, without the consent of the Owner nor in time of war, but in a manner to be prescribed by law.

Amendment IV.

The right of the people to be secure in their persons, houses, papers, and effects, against unreasonable searches and seizures, shall not be violated, and no Warrants shall issue, but upon probable cause, supported by Oath or affirmation, and particularly describing the place to be searched, and the persons or things to be seized.

Amendment V.

No person shall be held to answer for a capital, or otherwise infamous crime, unless on a presentment or indictment of a Grand Jury except in cases arising in the land or naval forces, or in the Militia, when in actual service in time of War or public danger; nor shall any person be subject for the same offence to be twice put in jeopardy of life or limb, nor shall be compelled in any criminal case to be a witness against himself, nor be deprived of life, liberty, or property, without due process of law; nor shall private property be taken for public use without just compensation.

Amendment VI.

In all criminal prosecutions, the accused shall enjoy the right to a speedy and public trial, by an impartial jury of the State and district wherein the crime shall have been committed; which district shall have been previously ascertained by law and to be informed of the nature and cause of the accusation; to be confronted with the witnesses against him; to have compulsory process for obtaining witnesses in his favor, and to have the assistance of counsel for his defence.

Amendment VII.

In Suits at common law where the value in controversy shall exceed twenty dollars, the right of trial by jury shall be preserved, and no fact tried by a jury shall be otherwise re-examined in any Court of the United States, than according to the rules of the common law.

Amendment VIII.

Excessive ball shall not be required, nor excessive fines imposed, nor cruel and unusual punishments inflicted.

Amendment IX.

The enumeration in the Constitution of certain rights shall not be construed to deny or disparage others retained by the people.

Amendment X.

The powers not delegated to the United States by the Constitution, nor prohibited by it to the States, are reserved to the States respectively, or to the people.

The first ten Amendments (BILL OF RIGHTS) were ratified effective December 15, 1791

Amendment XI.
Ratified February 7, 1795

The Judicial power of the United States shall not be construed to extend to any suit in law or equity, commenced or prosecuted against one of the United States by Citizens of another State, or by Citizens or Subjects of any Foreign State.

Amendment XII
Ratified June 15, 1804

The Electors shall meet in their respective states, and vote by ballot for President and Vice President, one of whom, at least, shall not be an inhabitant of the same state with themselves; they shall name in their ballots the person voted for as President, and in distinct ballots the person voted for as Vice-President, and they shall make distinct lists of all persons voted for as President, and of all persons voted for as Vice-President, and of the number of votes for each, which lists they shall sign and certify and transmit sealed to the seat of the government of the United States, directed to the President of the Senate; -The President of the Senate shall, in the presence of the Senate and House of Representatives, open all the certificates and the votes shall then be counted; -The person having the greatest number of votes for President, shall be the President, if such number be a majority of the whole number of Electors appointed; and if no person have such majority then from the persons having the highest numbers not exceeding three on the list of those voted for as President, the House of Representatives shall choose immediately, by ballot, the President. But in choosing the President, the votes shall be taken by states, the representation from each state having one vote; a quorum for this purpose shall consist of a member or members from two-thirds of the states, and a majority of all the states shall be necessary to a choice. [And if the House of Representatives shall not choose a President whenever the right of choice shall devolve upon them, before the fourth day of March next following, then the Vice President shall act as President, as in the case of the death or other constitutional disability of the President—] *(Superseded by Section 3 of the Twentieth Amendment)* The person having the greatest number of votes as Vice-President, shall be the Vice-President, if such number be a majority of the whole number of Electors appointed, and if no person have a majority, then from the two highest numbers on the list, the Senate shall choose the Vice-President; a quorum for the purpose shall consist of two-thirds of the whole number of Senators, and a majority of the whole number shall be necessary to a choice. But no person constitutionally ineligible to the office of President shall be eligible to that of Vice-President of the United States.

Amendment XIII
Ratified December 6, 1865

Section 1. Neither slavery nor involuntary servitude, except as a punishment for crime whereof the party shall have been duly convicted, shall exist within the United States, or any place subject to their jurisdiction.

Section 2. Congress shall have power to enforce this article by appropriate legislation.

Amendment XIV
Ratified July 9,1868

Section 1. All persons born or naturalized in the United States and subject to the jurisdiction thereof, are citizens of the United States and of the State wherein they reside. No State shall make or enforce any law which shall abridge the privileges or immunities of citizens of the United States; nor shall any State deprive any person of life, liberty, or property; without due process of law; nor deny to any person within its jurisdiction the equal protection of the laws.

Section 2. Representatives shall be apportioned among the several States according to their respective numbers, counting the whole number of persons in each State, excluding Indians not taxed. But when the right to vote at any election for the choice of electors for President and Vice President of the United States, Representatives in Congress, the Executive and Judicial officers of a State, or the members of the Legislature thereof, is denied to any of the male inhabitants of such State, being twenty-one years of age, and citizens of the United States, or in any way abridged, except for participation in rebellion, or other crime, the basis of representation therein shall be reduced in the proportion which the number of such male citizens shall bear to the whole number of male citizens twenty-one years of age in such State.

Section 3. No person shall be a Senator or Representative in Congress, or elector of President and Vice President, or hold any office, civil or military under the United States, or under any State, who, having previously taken an oath, as a member of Congress, or as an officer of the United States, or as a member of any State legislature, or as an executive or judicial officer of any State, to support the Constitution of the United States, shall have engaged in insurrection or rebellion against the same, or given aid or comfort to the enemies thereof. But Congress may by a vote of two-thirds of each House, remove such disability.

Section 4. The validity of the public debt of the United States, authorized by law, including debts incurred for payment of pensions and bounties for services in suppressing insurrection or rebellion, shall not be questioned. But neither the United States nor any State shall assume or pay any debt or obligation incurred in aid of insurrection or rebellion against the United States, or any claim for the loss or emancipation of any slave; but all such debts, obligations and claims shall be held illegal and void.

Section 5. The Congress shall have power to enforce, by appropriate legislation, the provisions of this article.

APPENDIX A

Search	Justification Necessary to Support
Inventory	Administrative Regulation
Administrative	Administrative Regulation with Guidelines
Search Persons in an Automobile	Reasonable Suspicion
Stop and Frisk	Reasonable Suspicion
Interior of Auto	Reasonable Suspicion and Fear for Safety
Arrest	Probable Cause
Warrantless Arrest	Probable Cause to Arrest
Warrantless Search	Probable Cause to Search
Interior of Auto and Containers	Probable Cause to Arrest or Reasonable Suspicion
Entire Auto including Containers	Probable Cause to Search

Table of Cases

Index

A

B

C

F

G

I